High Praise for Ed Chaffin and
UnCommon Leadership® for the New Reality

"This book is timely and critical. Filled with engaging stories and practical advice to use today, *UnCommon Leadership® for the New Reality* will equip you with the tools that you need for inspiring leadership, no matter how long you've been a leader."

—Marshall Goldsmith, Thinkers50 #1 Executive Coach, New York Times bestselling author of *Triggers, Mojo, and What Got You Here Won't Get You There*

"Today's world is demanding caring and inspirational leaders capable of bringing out the best in their teams and organizations. In *UnCommon Leadership®*, Chaffin helps you uncover your leadership tendencies and refine your leadership style to best serve those in your span of care. An exceptional resource for anyone looking to elevate humanity by making great leadership common practice!"

—Bob Chapman, CEO of Barry-Wehmiller, author of *Everybody Matters: The Extraordinary Power of Caring for Your People Like Family*

"As the leader of a community mental health center, I am keenly aware of the impact our New Reality is having on our communities and employees across all sectors. Ed distills the workplace chaos of these pandemic years and successfully identifies the simple, not easy, path forward for all of us as we lead ourselves and our organizations into and through the New Reality. This is a must-read for leadership teams everywhere."

— Lisa A. Dominisse, President and CEO, Grant Blackford Mental Health, Inc.

"The path to finding our unique leadership style is probably the most adventurous journey of our life and full of paradoxes. We are challenged to discover who we are at our core while recognizing that the road will partly remain a beautiful mystery. Knowing ourselves is a process of encounters with other people: leadership does not exist in a vacuum. This book is very special, for Ed has woven an extremely rich thread of wisdom that builds on his experience in working with people from around the globe. *UnCommon Leadership® for the New Reality* is also unique for it shines light on deeper, less visible layers of ourselves such as the grief that is in our hearts, minds, and bodies and that shapes our identities and thus our leadership. Ed dares to lead the way not because he has all the answers on how to best deal with the challenges our lives present to us but because he knows what questions to ask. And this is precisely where the real depth and wisdom of this book is to be found. Being a leader is allowing your full humanity to be revealed and thus permitting others to do the same. Ed is going all that way throughout his own life. Shall we join him? One-size-fits-all leadership is dead!"

—Jakob van Wielink, Partner,
De School voor Transite, Netherlands

"Ed Chaffin is a genius. This book is a helluva good read. It is packed with wisdom, insights, tips, and strategies that can help all of us become uncommon, impactful leaders. Read it. Remember it. Use it!"

—Terry Small, AKA The Brain Guy, Vancouver

"Ed Chaffin's *UnCommon Leadership® for the New Reality* is a timely and essential reading for any leader who wants to thrive in today's world of empowered employees who demand much more from their leaders. It is an insightful, practical guide to becoming a beloved inspirational leader who respects, motivates, and empowers people to achieve greatness together. UnCommon Leadership gives us an exhilarating and powerful roadmap to achieve leadership excellence in the New Reality by focusing on core beliefs, a clear vision, and genuine understanding of oneself and others. It is the antidote to the antiquated one-size-fits-all leadership of the past, paving the way for *'many sizes fit most,'* relationship-centric leadership for the New Reality. Implementing the advice in this book will make us all better leaders and better human beings. I am grateful to Ed for sharing his decades of accumulated UnCommon Wisdom to help us become enduring UnCommon Leaders in a rapidly changing world."

—John Pavlidis, CEO, Entrepreneur, Coach, and Lifelong Student

"I have known Ed for several years. He has put in this book what I have seen him model in both his personal and professional life. I was fascinated to learn about the science behind our belief system and how that shapes us! It is not just theory to Ed. He has actually done what he describes in this book with great success. This book will give you the reason to lead and the kick in the pants to start implementing a real change in yourself…which will lead to a change in your team!"

—Brad Thomas, Partner, Fried Goldberg, LLC

"Ed Chaffin hits at the heart of what leaders need to succeed in the post-Covid New Reality. He reveals how self awareness, vision, and the ability to personalize leadership are key to employee engagement and leader success. Chaffin's vivid storytelling and relevant examples are sure to resonate with seasoned leaders and newcomers. Rooted in his personal executive leadership journey and career as a top rated global executive coach, his lessons are both practical and thought provoking. I highly recommend this book to anyone ready to step up and embrace the next level of "UnCommon Leadership."

—Marcie Mueller, VP Global Leadership Development,
IMPACT Group

"In *UnCommon Leadership® for the New Reality,* Ed Chaffin has developed the three main principles very clearly, simply, and smartly. He provides personal stories throughout the book as well as very powerful quotes, such as the one from *Alice in Wonderland*, that amplify the teaching and learning for each chapter. Ed's writing style is dynamic, well documented, and a really lively read. And, you know what? This book is the right one at the right TIME, after the pandemic and given all the questions we have even more of now as leaders. The book contains inspirational vision for every reader and it's time to embrace the changes Ed is recommending."

—Carine Paumier-Hug, Managing Director,
Wabtec/Vapor Rail, Montreal

"Ed wisely makes the case that establishing employees' psychological safety is vitally important for leaders in the uncertain post-pandemic working world. But no one teaches them how to do it. This book is a roadmap from a man who has done it brilliantly as a leader, and as an external advisor. Highly recommended!"

—Dan King, Co-Founder,
Fireside Strategic and Fireside Private Equity

"This is a groundbreaking book, simple, straightforward, and easy to read. It's required reading for leaders who want to achieve groundbreaking results along with their teams in this New Reality."

**—Francisco D'Angelo, Partner, Coaching International,
and Former CEO, Yobel SCM, Peru**

"I first met Ed Chafin during my MBA and am proud to call him my friend, colleague, mentor, and personal coach. He is the definition of the 'consummate, servant leader.' He has spent his career developing, living, and sharing his principles on leadership which are based on the philosophy of 'personalized leadership.' Based on his teachings, I have been able to lead surgical teams more effectively in my career as a Vascular Surgeon.

Ed's current book, *Uncommon Leadership® for the New Reality*, is the culmination of a life's work in the leadership arena. He accurately notes that the Covid-19 pandemic 'New Reality' is changing every leader and has been a wakeup call for all of us to reexamine our leadership principles. He points out the hard truths about leadership that the pandemic has put front and center:

- "One-size fits all" leadership will not work
- Leadership must be personal and personalized
- Three essential principles must be the foundation for leadership—self leadership, vision, and personal and personalized leadership

Now, more than ever, we need to incorporate Ed's leadership values into our own leadership philosophy. I recommend this book to anyone in a leadership position as a *foundation* for developing and improving one's leadership style and effectiveness."

—John G Adams, Jr, MD, MBA, FACS, FSVS

"This book is fascinating. Ed Chaffin makes the case that good leadership today is personal and personalized. He lays out, with passion and authenticity, the principles that enable us to do just that: find our own distinctive way so that people follow us, not because they must, but because they want to. If you want to help this world act braver and better, this book is a must read."

—**Petra Reindl, Head of Global People & Executive Development, Munich Re, Germany**

"Ed Chaffin's book is a leadership guide that is long overdue. In my own leadership journey as a CEO for 22 years, which evolved into a successful executive coaching practice, I've read a ton of books and articles on leadership. *UnCommon Leadership® for the New Reality* gets to the heart of leadership—i.e., the behaviors and mindset leaders must embrace for sustainable success. It is a great mix of research, storytelling, and Ed's own lessons from his decades of leadership. I found it as readable as it is inspiring, and most importantly, it is filled with actionable insights for today's leadership needs."

—**Craig S. Juengling, PCC, Executive Coach, top 5% coaching practice worldwide**

"Ed's book *UnCommon Leadership® for the New Reality* spells out learned leadership principles that are timely given the fundamental shift in thought the workforce is undergoing as they evaluate their relationship with work. As a consultant, Ed was able to help us navigate through the importance of establishing and communicating vision, both personally and professionally, while challenging our perceptions of leadership. His unique experiences in business and expertise in understanding people through his Birkman training have shaped how we invest in our team, and the impacts have been tremendous."

—**Lance Dillard, CEO, Verifent**

"Ed Chaffin came to IMPACT Group in 2014 as my president, and I saw firsthand his dedication and commitment to driving a level of leadership that focuses on people first. His book provides a roadmap for any aspiring leader as to the important principles that drive the kind of leadership the post-pandemic world needs. His transparent and authentic writing style will capture your attention as he takes you on the journey of discovering how to become an UnCommon Leader!"

—Lauren Herring, CEO/Owner, IMPACT Group

"Ed worked with our leadership team at a cyber security startup that I co-founded, and we were flush with varying levels of leadership and aligning on vision. Following the teamwork that we did, Ed continued to work with me as an executive coach helping me navigate all the challenging situations I faced as a young leader. I will always remember the phrase 'Put the fish on the table,' and I continue to use it today! He is a master at quickly identifying leadership challenges and bringing them to light in a collaborative manner, and in his book *UnCommon Leadership® for the New Reality* he brings many of the ideas and principles about leadership that I and our leadership experienced. I highly recommend the book!"

—Colby DeRodeff, CTO, Mandiant Advantage

"*UnCommon Leadership® for the New Reality* is a concentrated load of life wisdom, understandable and structured. A gift, this openness and honesty with which Ed captivates his readership."

—Sabine Fercher, CEO, Fercher Compliance, Switzerland

"Based on his own stories and experiences Ed Chaffin offers sound advice as well as practical tips and examples for emerging and existing leaders to help realize their innate greatness to become "the best version" of themselves. In order to reach a new level of leadership for ourselves and others, successful education does not stop with university graduation. Based on his extensive experience as an executive, consultant, and coach as well as on his exorbitant interest in people, Chaffin owns the unparalleled talent to make leadership development more tangible by extrapolating his three principles as fundamental lessons of leadership. With this book Chaffin will certainly guide and inspire future generations into becoming the best version of the leaders of tomorrow."

—Dr. Thorsten Thiel, CEO, Alanus Foundation, Germany

"In the past two years of living with Covid we have been constantly hearing about the desire for change in the ways we live and work. But how and what to change? Ed captures the essence of the issues facing many leaders today. That our vision and beliefs about ourselves and (the ever changing) environment around us affects leaders in many ways, some apparent, others in more subconscious ways. This drives perceptions or misperceptions. Ultimately, the quest for change must be guided and challenged by a keen awareness of our visions and beliefs."

—Paul Chan, CFO

"Ed so simply yet powerfully reminds us of what truly great and 'UnCommon Leaders' <u>believe</u>, at their core—that, 'It's not about me; it's about the people whom I'm blessed to serve!' The people we, as leaders, are blessed to serve yearn for leadership that is 'personal and personalized,' where meaning and purpose are brought to life through a compelling and inspirational <u>vision</u> grounded in foundational values that, together, provide 'hope for the future.' Surround yourself with role models and leaders like Ed that will help you lead in an UnCommon way. By doing so, you will 'elevate your leadership to become someone people will eagerly follow' for generations to come."

—Steve Hayes, an aspiring Servant Leader, Husband, Father, Grandfather, and Senior Managing Director, Gallagher Executive Search and Leadership Advisors.

"Finally, a book that helps leaders to lead in a post-Covid world. We've all read the studies and articles about the changes in our workforce and how things will never be the same, but they only increase anxiety in leaders. Ed's timely and useful book helps leaders uncover their own internal wisdom and lead in an authentic way that will result in better retention and better profits."

—Brenda Abdilla, PCC, Author of *Outsmarting Crazytown: A Business Novel About How Derailed Professionals Can Get Back On Track*

"Ed was my first executive coach who helped me find my strengths and shore up some weaknesses. This book oozes with Ed's insights and -isms. My favorite story in the book is of his pep talk with his new team about People + Process = Profits because I got the same pep talk that helped me refocus on people in a way that had a profitable outcome. In this book he uses terms like New Reality, UnCommon Leadership, and Platinum Rule very effectively. Pay attention because what he is really telling us is that happy employees will make happy clients and that will drive profitable results. And you can't change your behavior if you don't first look at and change your beliefs on how you are leading your people today. I appreciate Ed putting his life's work into this book and I hope you will read it and learn from it in your effort to Stay Curious, which is my favorite Edism."

—Doug Lawyer-Smith, Founder & CEO, Sweetwork—Better Work. More Life.

"This must-read book gave me a new and more complete understanding of leadership. Any leader looking to strengthen their teams and accelerate results should get to know Ed Chaffin's UnCommon Leadership® approach. It is required reading for any leader looking to play to her or his strengths and inspire others to win."

—Dr. Alexander Zinser, Roy C. Hitchman AG,
Executive Search, Partner

"This book is a must-read for anyone who wants to be a great leader! Ed Chaffin provides a simple set of steps, supported by data and science to help us reset our personal GPS to arrive at a new level of successful leadership. He brilliantly tells us to start with a clear and unambiguous understanding of our personal values as a rock-solid foundation. Other books provide well-intentioned supportive ideas, while this book brings it all together. Put Ed's steps to work now!"

—Rick Walker, CEO, Attorney, Corporate Board Director

"Like a missive from the front lines, Ed has identified and elegantly illustrated the ways in which the essential nature of work has changed and how leaders will need to adapt to be effective. This is not a set of tips and tricks but an essential mindset shift that will serve as a sustainable foundation of leadership in a rapidly changing world."

—Peter Meyers, CEO, Stand & Deliver

"Ed generously shares his leadership journey to help us all navigate our New Reality. The book is highly actionable and easily digestible—so necessary in this attention-starved environment. His stories and illustrations help you get to the heart of the matter and grow your own leadership!"

—David Goldsmith, Executive Director, 7 Paths Forward, Co-founder, Accelerating Coaching Excellence

"In the Introduction, Ed Chaffin tells the story of going to the whiteboard. He essentially says, 'You'll enable people to become the best version of themselves.' That is a simple yet profound statement of leadership. I love this and the idea that we're not to try to make round pegs fit into square holes. I also loved the paradox of 'whether you believe you can or believe you can't, you're right.' Elevating belief as a powerful force and backing it up with epigenetics showing that we can change our beliefs and therefore our reality is a powerful concept to grab hold of as a human and a leader. *UnCommon Leadership® for the New Reality* provides the hope that we can become better leaders and in this book Ed gives a great framework on how to grow as a leader."

—Scott Noble, CFO, Wealth Without Regrets

"Ed Chaffin's new book, *Uncommon Leadership® for the New Reality: 3 Principles that Drive Greater Awareness, Engagement, and Psychological Safety*, is a timely resource for employers as the dust clears from Covid only to reveal a landscape where the 'War for Talent' has taken center stage and new ways of thinking about timeless principles are required. Mr. Chaffin's book is a fine contribution to meeting this need."

—Allen Hauge, Group Chair, Vistage

"In a world chock full of business books, Ed Chaffin takes a deeper cut. *Uncommon Leadership® for the New Reality* offers a competitive edge for those who are willing to look at their own beliefs, values, vision, and understanding of self. With 'Points to Remember' at the end of every chapter and personal stories that bring the principles to life, Ed takes the reader on a journey of personal and personalized leadership, reminding us that leading starts by looking within."

—Marie Elena Rigo, MA, President, MER Leadership Design

UnCommon Leadership®

for the
New Reality

3 Principles that Drive Greater Awareness, Engagement, and Psychological Safety

ED CHAFFIN, PCC

Publishing support provided by
Ignite Press
5070 N. Sixth St. #189
Fresno, CA 93710
www.IgnitePress.us

ISBN: 979-8-9861749-0-7
ISBN: 979-8-9861749-1-4 (Hardcover)
ISBN: 979-8-9861749-2-1 (E-book)

For bulk purchase and for booking, contact:

Ed Chaffin
ed@edchaffin.com
15405 Holcombe Dr.
Westfield, IN 46074

Scriptures marked KJV are taken from the KING JAMES VERSION (KJV): KING JAMES VERSION, public domain.

Library of Congress Control Number: 2022907587

Cover design by Aasman Iqbal
Chief Editor – Peter Lundell and 2nd Editor Charlie Wormhoudt
Interior design by Eswari Kamireddy

FIRST EDITION

F2

This book is dedicated to my wife Eva, whose unconditional love for over 40 years has inspired me to be the best version of myself that I could be. Without her support and encouragement this book and all that I've been able to accomplish in life would have never happened.

And to my three children; Stacy, Brett, and Erica, and their spouses Dow, Patsy, and Justin. I failed at being a father many times, but they have challenged me and inspired me to keep moving forward and realize that life is a journey and not an event. I am blessed beyond measure to have them all in my life.

And, to Jade—the best "grand doggie" that I could have ever had. May she rest in peace after over 19 years of bringing love and joy to me and our family!

CONTENTS

Foreword xix

Preface xxi

Introduction: The Uncommon Leadership® Journey 1

PRINCIPLE 1 - LEADERSHIP STARTS WITH YOUR BELIEFS 13

CHAPTER 1: The Biology of Belief 15

CHAPTER 2: Where Do Our Beliefs Originate? 23

CHAPTER 3: The Battle Between our Conscious and
Subconscious Minds 33

CHAPTER 4: What Do You Believe About You? 39

CHAPTER 5: Rewiring Our Brains for New Beliefs 45

CHAPTER 6: What Do You Believe about Other People? 57

CHAPTER 7: What Do You Believe about Change and
the Connection To Talent Development? 63

PRINCIPLE 2 - LEADERSHIP REQUIRES 20/20 VISION 73

CHAPTER 8: Do You Know Where You're Going? 75

CHAPTER 9: Start With Your Values 83

CHAPTER 10: Defining Your Values 89

CHAPTER 11: Creating the Vision 93

CHAPTER 12: Communicating Your Vision 99

CHAPTER 13: The Difference Between Mission and
Vision Statements 105

CHAPTER 14: Trust, Compassion, Stability, and Hope 109

PRINCIPLE 3 - LEADERSHIP IS IN THE EYE OF THE BEHOLDER **113**

CHAPTER 15: Leadership Requires New Thinking for
the New Reality 115

CHAPTER 16: The Sock-Sock, Shoe-Shoe Story 119

CHAPTER 17: Your Presence and Your Energy Matter 123

CHAPTER 18: Reading the Label—How Do We Really Know
How We Lead? 129

CHAPTER 19: Brain-Based Leadership—Psychological
Safety Drives Connectivity 135

CHAPTER 20: How Much Should a Leader Care? 143

CHAPTER 21: Leadership and Management Styles 149

CHAPTER 22: Why Do We Miss Leading Others?
Our Intrinsic Motivations Are Hidden! 157

CHAPTER 23: Harnessing the Power of the Team 169

Final Thought 175
Endnotes 181
Acknowledgments 191
About the Author 201

FOREWORD

Being a leader is difficult. No debate about this. And being an excellent leader is far more difficult. For this reason, there have been thousands of books aiming to help us find better ways to walk this challenging path. Now, as we emerge from the global pandemic, leaders face an unpredictable environment where, in a complex global market, digital technology increasingly dominates our lives. If we're to survive and improve as leaders, we must be willing to embrace this change. With a new set of ground rules for the workplace, we must learn to lead in a world that is demanding a new approach to leadership.

For such a time as this, we're fortunate that Ed Chaffin, a seasoned corporate leader and executive coach, has assembled in these pages a content-rich and valuable leadership guide. In his book *UnCommon Leadership® for the New Reality* Ed covers ground on a variety of leadership topics as he shares his insights from his impressive career of leading from inside as president and from the outside as a consultant, executive coach, and mentor.

I am particularly grateful that Ed Chaffin, who has been an exceptional Birkman-certified professional for many years, chose to conclude this book with a focus on our assessment, The Birkman Method®. Ed explains that, while leading with the Golden Rule is good, leading with the Platinum Rule is far more powerful and effective when it comes to leadership.

If this is the case, then how do we apply the Platinum Rule?

The first two principles of this book offer richly detailed answers to this question, beginning with *Leadership Starts with Your Beliefs* and *Leadership Requires 20/20 Vision.* Ed then brings it all together with a roadmap for exactly what is meant by *Leadership is in the Eye of the Beholder* and explains how the Birkman Method provides this information and the application for you.

In the early 1950s, my father realized something new in the field of social psychology by capturing the power of our social perceptions. He did this in a way that allows leaders to see their own leadership style more accurately and, *perhaps even more importantly, to see the needs of others in a way that is unique to the Birkman Method.* Most personality tests offer self-awareness, but leaders know, that's only half the story, like looking through only one eye. The Birkman Method has endured for seven decades by revealing the motivating needs of your followers.

If you're a leader now, or hope to one day be a leader, read this book. It's the gift of Ed's wisdom and advice that will speed you on your way to becoming an outstanding and UnCommon Leader.

Sharon Birkman
CEO, Birkman International, Houston, TX

PREFACE

arch 2020. Do you remember that month? By that time most of us had heard about the COVID-19 virus. We had a lot of uncertainty, and it appeared we might be heading into a pandemic. But what did that mean? We were soon to find out. And at the time few of us could have imagined how our lives would be disrupted. Do you remember where you were when you first realized that this epidemic talk was becoming a reality that would radically change the life you had been living up to that time?

In the beginning, a massive amount of new and different information was coming in waves of increasing frequency. By the first week of March, people who work for a major company in Indianapolis were already working from home because one of their employees had attended a biotech conference in Boston that turned out to be a super-spreader event. Other companies were starting to shut down, and every leader of every company was soon to make some of the same tough decisions.

For me, March 4 was to be the start of a work-driven, five-week, domestic and international travel schedule that included bringing my wife, Eva, on the international segments as she and I were heading to Prague and Vienna to celebrate our 39th wedding anniversary in between work assignments. At about 6 p.m. ET on March 3 I said to her, "I guess I'm on a plane tomorrow to head to California since I haven't heard from my client."

She replied, "Well, it's only 3 p.m. in California, so there's still time to hear from them."

At 7:05 p.m. the phone rang, and sure enough, it was my California client, who said, "Don't get on the plane tomorrow. We're locking down the offices and sending everyone home. I'm not sure when we'll get back in the office, so let's stay in touch." Over two years later and we still haven't rescheduled the team program I was contracted to do.

Almost all of our worlds—all over the world—were turned upside down. And I'm sure that most of you have similar stories of those points in time when life as you knew it was being flipped upside down for you and your family, friends, and co-workers.

Little did we know that years later we would still be dealing with this Covid situation, particularly the resurgences, on a global basis. The 2020 Tokyo Summer Olympics were delayed a year, then held without fans in attendance, followed by the audience-free stands of the Beijing Winter Olympics. It seemed a sacrilege, but that's what we dealt with. And athletes tell us that they feed off the energy of the crowds. Later, to see major sporting events with stadiums full of fans was incredibly liberating.

It seems we are so close to being back to normal. But of course, there seems to be no such thing as normal anymore. I call it the *New Reality*. We all must deal with it and determine how to move forward in our lives and careers.

Though some areas of life have gone back to the way they were, regarding our work and our careers, a New Reality has definitively emerged. Josh Bersin, who at the time was associated with Deloitte consulting, stated in his "Predictions for 2014," regarding the war for talent that had been predicted by McKinsey since 1997, that the war was over, and talent had won.[1]

We now see that statement being magnified exponentially in ways we could not have previously imagined. The endless, widespread stories of employees saying they will never go back to the industry they were in or that they will never go back to working in an office is staggering.

Most days I read at least one article about what employees and companies are saying about their work environment and reopening offices. Some companies are asking employees to come back to the office without understanding their employees' intrinsic motivations. Employees are saying, "I'm in control, and I'm going to focus on my mental, emotional, and physical health over working for the man." The bottom line is that the New Reality is challenging every leader today in ways we couldn't have imagined a short time ago.

Some leaders are realizing the New Reality as they step up and provide many options for their employees about where and how they work. I see conflicting news reports in the media that say there has been no loss of productivity and that there has been a loss of productivity. Obviously, a lot of results are determined by the industry and ultimately the leadership of a given company as to what their New Reality is.[2]

Unfortunately, we have countless examples of what I believe are tone-deaf leaders dictating the terms for returning to their offices, and the backlash from employees can be extreme. For companies such as JP Morgan Chase and Goldman Sachs, the message is, we are in charge, and if you want to work for us, you're going to come to an office. Some companies think they are making great decisions by going hybrid with a mix of working at home and working in the office. But they haven't stopped to realize that this one-size-fits-all mentality won't work anymore.

One great example of this is Apple. I'm a huge Apple fan and user of their products. But Tim Cook initially announced unilaterally that employees were expected to be in the office three days a week and gave a return date for the execution of that plan. The cacophony of noise from a large group of employees was almost instantaneously negative. Some of these employees had moved away from Silicon Valley to take advantage of better and cheaper housing, and they were not about to go back to the office, even for one day a week. Ultimately, Cook had to rescind the initial edict and as we go to print that initiative has been put on hold.[3]

Another point that has entered the arena and the conversation is about mental and emotional well-being. It's finally okay to admit that you're not okay. If Covid did nothing else for us, it opened the door for honest dialogue about the fact that so many of us struggle from time to time. And Covid showed us that employers and companies need to be open to that conversation and that employees need to address it and not cover up their emotions and pretend they're okay.

If you are a regular user of the business social media site LinkedIn, then you have seen the abundance of postings and articles from people who are sharing deep, personal stories of tragedy and triumph. And many of the postings have nothing to do with Covid. It is people telling their story of overcoming drug addictions, abusive relationships, deep, dark depressions, and many other obstacles they have overcome. Why are they doing this now? To give hope to desperate people as the chaos that has entered lives and workplaces is very hard to quantify. It seems that no topic regarding mental and physical health is taboo at this point. And one area Covid has exposed that could take me down a deep rabbit hole is the issue of bereavement leave. I'm sorry corporations and leaders, three days to deal with the loss of a close loved one is just ridiculous! Especially when some people experienced the loss of a loved one during Covid and weren't permitted to say goodbye!

The loss and grief from losing a loved one doesn't just affect the employee. It affects everyone around them, including the people they work with and the company.

Here's the point: *Never in the history of the employment market have employees been more in charge and dictating the terms of their work.* Their New Reality is that they are in charge, and they aren't going to take it any longer. They're saying: "Boss, you either pay attention to me as an individual and a human being, or I'm gone."

This book was in process for more than a year, and the truth is I kept getting stuck. Some legitimate obligations necessitated my focus on other things, but I also had this voice telling me I wasn't on the right track. One thing I've learned over the years is to listen to that voice and let it be okay to wait and see how things unfold. For an action-oriented, make-it-happen person, this has been a huge struggle, but numerous experiences showed me why waiting was the prudent action. The Covid situation has caused me to realize that the method of leadership I've lived and taught and coached for the past 18 years—that leadership is personal and person-alized—has never been more needed in our companies.

We've had many leadership movements through the years, from the old days of MBO (Managing by Objectives) to Primal Leadership (Dan Goleman's research and work), to Servant Leadership, Situational Leadership, and one of my favorites, Truly Human Leadership, brought to the world through Bob Chapman, the Chairman/CEO of Barry Wehmiller. The shift and the deeper insight that UnCommon Leadership® brings to the conversation is to recognize that even if we adopt one of the above-mentioned leadership styles, is it being done with the view of the Platinum Rule, which is the essence and foundation for personal and personalized leadership?

One of my mentors was the incredible Dr. Roger Birkman, creator of the Birkman Method® assessment. He taught me and other Birkman consultants that there was a better way than the Golden Rule. Most of us know what that is, but to make sure here is the definition: *Do unto others as you would have them do unto you.*

But think about it. What *I* want and need—my intrinsic motivations—may be very different from *yours.* So if you lead the way you want to be led, you might be missing the mark with some of the people that you lead. The Platinum Rule makes this shift: *Do unto others as they would want to be done unto them.*

This is exactly what is being played out in labor markets around the world, especially in the US. You see, the three leadership principles you'll read about in this book are ones I've used in speeches, workshops, and webinars for a long time, and I have used them personally in key leadership roles. In using these principles, I've seen the results first hand and know they work. Codifying and making the information available to a broader audience at this key point in time has been the final motivation for me to move forward and finish writing this book.

Leaders should realize the chaos that their employees are experiencing. In fact, the leadership and consulting organization Korn Ferry published an article indicating that companies should hire two new employees for this New Reality—a chief chaos officer and a chief wellbeing officer. The chief wellbeing officer is more common in Europe, but not so much in the US and other countries.[4]

Korn Ferry's article vividly points out that we need a new way of thinking about leadership. *UnCommon Leadership® for the New Reality* sets out to identify what each of us can do personally to adapt and move forward in a more honest, caring, and productive manner.

THE UNCOMMON LEADERSHIP® JOURNEY

I've always been interested in leadership and how a person can become a leader that inspires others. In retracing how that desire was birthed in my childhood, I believe that the origin was in church, watching my father give a 30-minute sermon and seeing people decide to do something that for most of them was life changing. He was a bit relentless in his pursuit sometimes, and if you know anything about Protestant faiths, especially Southern Baptists, the only day worth preaching was a day that saw someone come down the aisle and profess their new-found faith in Christ. We would sing 42 verses of "Just As I Am," and I would be in the back of the church, praying someone would finally heed the call so we could go home and watch Sunday afternoon baseball. Turning on the TV to watch the baseball coverage with Pee Wee Reese and Dizzy Dean was what I lived for on Sundays—not the sermon.

Fast forward to the year 2004. I had been with a company since early 1995, and we were on a roll. We had gone public in 1996, and after a few fits and starts we were attracting a lot of attention from the investment community and doing well. In 2002 we started an acquisition binge and by 2004 had acquired four companies in the area of unemployment cost management. We created a new division and originally asked one of the acquired executives to run that division, but it became obvious that wasn't the long-term strategy.

Our CEO met with me and said, "Ed, I'd like for you to take over the unemployment cost management division as its president." While I had a significant role on our leadership team at the time, the thought of running that division was the furthest thing from my mind.

I said back to him, "Are you crazy?"

He proceeded to remind me that he knew what he was doing, and all I had to do was look around the company at how we had grown, how we had completely rearchitected ourselves from being a hardware and software company to being an application service provider (now known as SaaS), and the success we were having.

I agreed with him that he did know what he was doing, but he also said something that changed my life. He said, "Ed, I know you can do this. You are the right person for this role. People trust you, and I trust you. You've been a valuable member of our leadership team, and I need you to do this. If it doesn't work out, we'll find a place for you."

How could I say no to that offer?

When I think back to that time, it was monumental for several reasons. I believed that I had been preparing for that challenge all my life, and it was time to put into practice what I believed about leadership. The essence of that belief is that it's not about me; it's about the people whom I'm blessed to serve. It's about making a difference in the lives of those whom my leadership team and I would lead. Some would call that belief "servant leadership." And yes, that was my objective in my leadership roles—making it about the people that I was leading. Over the next few years that belief would get transformed to another level as represented by the ideas you'll read in this book.

The day came for me to address the leadership team and direct reports I would inherit when I became president of what was then called UCeXpress, which had become, through acquisitions, the largest unemployment cost management company in the United States.

In the room was our CEO, the man I was replacing, and about 30 leaders whom I would lead from that day forward. I had prepared a speech about my vision, philosophies about my leadership mandate, and how I wanted to lead that division.

It went something like this: "Most every one of you on this leadership team has come from a privately held company, and the shift to working for a publicly traded company has been a challenge. I'm convinced that some of you think EPS [earnings per share] is a four-letter dirty word. Here's my commitment to you as your new leader. If you will follow me and embrace the direction I believe we should go, here's how we're going to approach this effort."

I hadn't planned to write anything, but as I was saying these words, I grabbed a marker and went to the whiteboard because it occurred to me that a visual of what I was about to say would be helpful to connect the words.

I wrote on the whiteboard in big letters the word PEOPLE. "I believe that people are our number one asset, and if we take care of our people, they will take care of our clients. My commitment is that we will invest in them beyond just the knowledge they need to do their jobs. We will help them become better people and better leaders, which will enable them to be the best version of themselves they can be."

I then wrote a plus sign followed by the word PROCESS. "At the same time that we focus on our people, we will also look at every process that we have. We receive over four million pieces of mail every year, and we must examine our processes to see where we can become more efficient and improve our quality as our customers depend on us to get it right."

I then wrote an equal sign and the word PROFITS. "I believe if we follow this formula—focus on our people and focus on our processes—the profits will follow. And here's one more commitment. I will not beat you over the head about EPS because I believe the profits will follow if we do the right things."

With that, I looked at my new leadership team and asked, "I'm ready to go to work. Are you with me?"

I don't remember the exact reactions or what anyone specifically said, but I do remember the looks on their faces. I could see they were inspired, and they were ready to go to work with a different way of thinking about our business. After the meeting as I walked down the hall toward my new office, the man I was replacing, who had been in the room, commented, "That was an incredible speech, Ed. I think I'm ready to go to work for you!" Coming from a man with whom I had experienced some significant challenges due to his leadership style, that was a high compliment.

The journey was now at a point where what I had read, studied, and believed would be put to the test. The amazing thing is that the leadership team I had inherited bought the vision and the mandate—*focus on people and process*.

The esprit de corps on our team was incredible, and over the next four years we built one of the most highly engaged groups of people I've ever worked with. After some additional acquisitions in my division, we ended up with more than 1,200 employees in seven offices around the US, and 800 of those employees were hourly employees. We were able to create career paths for the different roles in our division so that even the $10-per-hour mailroom clerk knew what her career path could look like. We had numerous stories of finding those hourly employees that were "diamonds in the rough" and seeing them succeed, get promoted, and improve their income and their socio-economic status. When we hired new hourly employees, we could point at different people in the company and tell their stories of success and how we became a great place to work.

When I officially retired from that company in the summer of 2008, there were a lot of farewell lunches and dinners, and one was with the team of my direct reports that had been alongside me throughout the journey. We had many great laughs and stories of our success. At one point, one of them asked, "Ed, how did you know what to do when you took over?"

I told her it had been the cumulative total of all that I had studied and learned and believed about leadership, and to finally get the opportunity to run a division and live out those principles was a golden moment I wasn't going to waste. I was all in. But then I told her and the whole team, "You're giving me way too much credit. The credit goes to you because you had a choice that day when I painted the vision for where we were going and how we would get there. You bought it, you came alongside me, and together we fulfilled that vision. You each had a choice, and if any one of you had made a different choice, we wouldn't be having this great celebration."

At my retirement I was only 56 years old. And because I hold the belief that I will never, ever retire completely, I knew there was something else in store for me. I believe that as long as I can give back and function cognitively, God has a purpose for me. And back then, as now, I intended to figure out what that might be.

My retirement also yielded a lot of emails with wonderful accolades, and they all touched me with their sincerity about the difference I had made in these people's lives—more than I had ever realized. Somehow, and I still don't know how, other than that it was the voice of God telling me, I knew that a key to my future was somewhere in those emails. I told my wife that exact statement. I printed off all the emails, stuck them in a folder, and said, "Eva, once things settle down from our move back to Atlanta, I'm going to sit down and read those emails because I believe they will give me insight into what the future holds for me and where I'm going next."

I believe that each of us is on this planet for a reason, and if we can figure out some semblance of that reason, then we should keep doing that as long as we're able.

That inspiration was embedded in me by my association and friendship with the man I mentioned in the preface, Dr. Roger Birkman. Dr. B., as those close to him called him, came to the office every day until he was 93! Two years prior to that, I interviewed him for a speech I was about to do, and I wanted to get a video of him for the group. I had set up my Flip video camera, and we engaged in a great conversation about his path for creating the assessment. I then asked him a question to which I already knew the answer: "Dr. Birkman, you come to the office every day. You're 91. Why?"

He leaned toward me and the camera and said, "Ed, when you love what you do, it's not work!"

When you love what you do it's not work. How many of us figure that out in time to live out our lives in a way that has purpose and meaning? From the bottom of my heart, I wish every living person could figure that out because I know what it did for me and my family when I figured that out for myself. In the second section of the book, I will cover in detail the process that I went through and provide some suggestions for how you too can figure out what your *why* is and what you're on planet Earth for.

I've long believed that I had a book in me, and through the years I've written several outlines of different books. The truth is, the book I've wanted to write has seemed like Mt. Everest, and I continued to delay writing it. But after I developed a speech that I began delivering, and receiving extremely positive feedback, I realized I had the genesis of this book.

This book is the sum of my career and executive roles, plus my post-retirement career as an international leadership consultant and executive coach. It also includes the feedback I've received from more than a thousand leaders I've worked with over the past two decades, as well as the studying and certifications that I've done in my new career.

Here's my belief, and I want to encourage you to have this same belief: If you will read, absorb, and apply what you learn from this book, you can change what's needed for you as a leader and elevate your leadership to become someone people will eagerly follow—or as the book title suggests, become an UnCommon Leader for this New Reality in which we now operate.

For most of us living and participating in the public domain, I believe we are in a crisis of leadership, and Covid has exposed the crisis in ways we couldn't have previously imagined. One of the most visible representations of this is seen in government officials and politicians from many countries, not just the US. It seems that we may be living in one of the most divisive eras of our human history. We are in desperate need of strong, honest, caring leaders.

The Covid crisis and the vacuum of leadership has manifested itself in the following data compiled recently by Gartner:[1]

WHAT EMPLOYEES SAY ABOUT HOW THE PANDEMIC HAS CHANGED THEIR FEELINGS ABOUT WORK AND LIFE

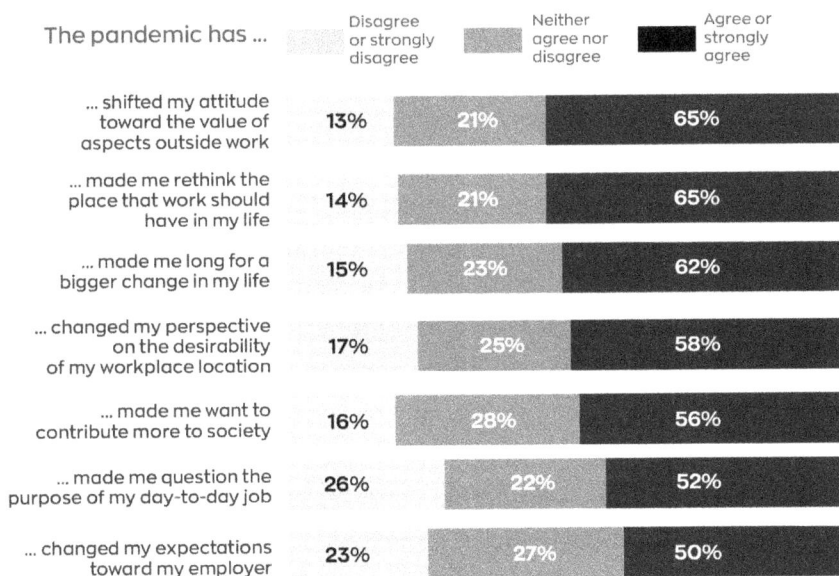

The pandemic has ...	Disagree or strongly disagree	Neither agree nor disagree	Agree or strongly agree
... shifted my attitude toward the value of aspects outside work	13%	21%	65%
... made me rethink the place that work should have in my life	14%	21%	65%
... made me long for a bigger change in my life	15%	23%	62%
... changed my perspective on the desirability of my workplace location	17%	25%	58%
... made me want to contribute more to society	16%	28%	56%
... made me question the purpose of my day-to-day job	26%	22%	52%
... changed my expectations toward my employer	23%	27%	50%

This is a quantum shift that people of the world are experiencing, and we must pay attention to the kind of information Gartner and many other studies have discovered. I can summarize their information this way: *Many people want meaning in their life and work, and they no longer want work to dominate their lives.*

The idea of work-life balance has shifted to life-work balance with people first and foremost wanting more from their lives. They are desperate for leaders who inspire and serve them in a way other than viewing them as widgets in the production model.

What makes this most important is that from my own experiences, finding and working with a leader you can trust and admire, who motivates and inspires you to be the best version of yourself, and who considers your well-being first and foremost, is a challenge. I have worked for, and with, very few leaders whom I would consider UnCommon Leaders—those who walk their talk, have high integrity, bring people together for the greater good, and practice a form of personal and personalized leadership where they recognize it's not about them but about the people they are blessed to work with and lead. That is a very sad statement to write, but I've quantified in interviews that many people feel the exact same way.

Are there great leaders in business and even our government? Yes. But there simply aren't enough of them. Or maybe there are but we just don't hear about them—which is part of the mission I'm on, to change that narrative. I am convinced we need a revolution of leadership where leaders understand what's important. And it's not them! Covid has provided the ultimate wake-up call for all leaders to realize that a massive shift is needed.

Leadership is a privilege, and that privilege requires commitment and dedication. It starts with self leadership, or personal leadership, and deeply examining who you are, what your strengths are, and how you affect others with your natural leadership style. It's also about others and the difference you can and will make in the lives of those you lead. I'll say it once more because I firmly believe it: If you will take the three principles presented in this book and apply them and live them out, you can elevate your leadership beyond where it is today. The information in this book is timeless and relevant for anyone, no matter what your age or employment position. The key, though, is that you can benefit from this information only if you apply it.

Here is a graphic of the three leadership principles you are about to discover and the key points of each section.

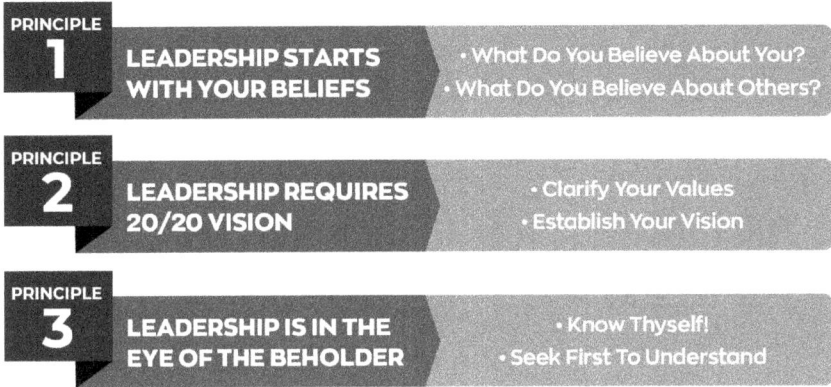

PRINCIPLE 1
LEADERSHIP STARTS WITH YOUR BELIEFS
• What Do You Believe About You?
• What Do You Believe About Others?

PRINCIPLE 2
LEADERSHIP REQUIRES 20/20 VISION
• Clarify Your Values
• Establish Your Vision

PRINCIPLE 3
LEADERSHIP IS IN THE EYE OF THE BEHOLDER
• Know Thyself!
• Seek First To Understand

All three of this book's principles grew out of feedback from the many people I've worked with and coached as well as my own executive leadership roles. In the first section, I'll cover the principle of our belief systems and include some revolutionary brain science about the biology of our beliefs. This is the foundation for everything. It's been said, "Whether you believe you can or believe you can't, you're right." We now have science to back up that statement. Is it really that simple? Yes, it is, but then we must understand the nature of the brain to realize why it isn't that simple either. It is a paradox, and grasping that, you'll have a better understanding of why sometimes we succeed and sometimes we don't.

The second section is driven by two factors. One is my own personal journey that I started in the early 1990s to discover what my Mission/Vision/Values were. Exploring and discovering a vision for yourself is fundamental to developing a "north star" to navigate your life and your destiny. The other factor is from an IBM study that identified a definitive source of employee engagement.[2] The two factors intersect in the discovery of what truly drives you and therefore what drives employee engagement.

My promise is that after discovering the true source of employee engagement, you will understand leadership in a very different way. The guarantee is that you will have a new and more complete understanding of leadership that will create an UnCommon Leadership® approach for you and the people that you lead, which will grow them into a following of highly engaged people.

In the third section, we'll cover the reality that leadership is defined by each of us in potentially very different ways. It truly is like beauty being in the eye of the beholder—leadership is in the eye of the beholder as well—both what you "behold" as your leadership style and what your followers "behold."

Another way of saying this, as I have been, is that leadership is personal and personalized. As the subheadings suggest, we must know who we are at deeper levels and how we affect others with our leadership styles. You'll discover a truth that has come back to me many times in the coaching and leadership work I've done: You are always leading whether you want to or not. One question with which I like to end a coaching session or a complete engagement is, "What are you taking away from our time together?" The answer I hear most often is, "I never realized that I'm always leading, no matter what." My favorite way of saying that statement is, "You're never not leading!"

Then we'll see how leadership requires knowing the intrinsic motivations of ourselves and the people that we are leading. I'll explore deeper the science of the brain and then introduce a leadership model developed from the research and writings of John Bowlby regarding "attachment theory" and explore why this is the key to developing a strong foundation of leadership that creates psychological safety for those we are working with and leading.

We'll also look into the shift of thinking that I referenced earlier and that will forever change your view of what leadership is about. It will transform your leadership from the Golden Rule to the Platinum Rule. I'll also cover in more detail why the Birkman Method® assessment that I've been using for more than 22 years is the most powerful method to give us specific and reliable information into who each of us is from a holistic standpoint. Each of us has intrinsic motivators that are needed for us to be the best version of ourselves and for our strengths to show up. And the Birkman Method provides that for us. I start all my executive coaching engagements and team projects with this assessment.

Great leaders learn that what motivates *me* may not motivate *you*, and they realize the need to develop personalized leadership versus one-size-fits-all leadership, which the Covid situation has revealed in stark terms.

I am positive that when you read that chapter in the book, you'll gain a different view on what personal and personalized leadership looks like. And I hope you will embrace this ethos of leadership, which is very specific for each one of us. In the speeches and workshops I do, I ask groups to describe leadership in one word. The answers are all very different. This gives us the clue about leadership's being in the eye of the beholder.

This last section presents a new lens for viewing your own leadership and, as I've stated before, is *the* critical factor in elevating your leadership beyond its current boundaries, or becoming an UnCommon Leader for our New Reality.

Are you ready to begin the journey of discovering and applying the principles for becoming an UnCommon Leader? If so, let's keep going!

LEADERSHIP STARTS WITH YOUR BELIEFS

PRINCIPLE 1	LEADERSHIP STARTS WITH YOUR BELIEFS	• What Do You Believe About You? • What Do You Believe About Others?
PRINCIPLE 2	LEADERSHIP REQUIRES 20/20 VISION	• Know Your Values • Establish Your Vision
PRINCIPLE 3	LEADERSHIP IS IN THE EYE OF THE BEHOLDER	• Know Thyself • Seek First to Understand

CHAPTER 1

THE BIOLOGY OF BELIEF

Genes and DNA do not control our biology.
Instead, DNA is controlled by signals from outside the cell,
including the energetic messages emanating from
our positive and negative thoughts.

— Bruce Lipton, Ph.D.

If we think about what the Covid situation has created, it has definitely led to people challenging some of our traditional belief systems. We've reexamined who we are, what we believe, and what we will do. Our beliefs are foundational for our success, and they drive our thoughts, our directions, and ultimately our destiny. The divisive war that went on about Covid and the right approach to fighting it demonstrated the power of our beliefs. This is why I start with our belief systems for examining leadership. It is the foundation on which all other conversations about being an UnCommon Leader rest.

Read the above quote one more time: "Genes and DNA do not control our biology. Instead, DNA is controlled by signals from outside the cell, including the energetic messages emanating from our positive and negative thoughts."[1] This idea is very important for us to establish a solid scientific foundation for examining our beliefs before we dive into our personal belief systems. This is foundational to our success, and too many times I've read articles or books that jump right into the idea of how powerful our beliefs are, yet they don't lay the groundwork to establish the science to back up these ideas. Without the science it's just a great idea and concept that is easy to dismiss or even get frustrated with.

Over the past few years I've read two books that have had a tremendous effect on me and provide the brain-based, scientific, biological information that has transformed our thinking about DNA, energy, and the brain. The first, quoted above, is Dr. Bruce Lipton's *The Biology of Belief: Unleashing the Power of Consciousness, Matter, and Miracles.* The second book is Dawson Church's, *Mind to Matter: The Astonishing Science of How Your Brain Creates Material Reality.* Church addresses and adds studies to confirm what Lipton wrote—that our thoughts literally influence matter.[2] I'll note Lipton's discoveries here and Church's in the third section.

Lipton discusses the science of epigenetics. In the process of examining his beliefs, he faced major rejection from those in the microbiology world. Epigenetics may be a new terminology for most people. It is also revolutionary.

When I am doing a speech or workshop on leadership, very few people raise their hands when I ask them if they've heard the term epigenetics. In a room of 100 people maybe five hands will go up, which is astonishing when considering that in 2004 this concept was reported by the *Wall Street Journal*, and Lipton codified it in his book in 2006. In fact, in 2016, Lipton released the tenth-anniversary edition of the book, which added much additional breakthrough scientific evidence.

Even though the science has been available in the public domain, it has not made its way into the realm and application of leadership and talent development practices. I believe it is ground-breaking in potentially unlocking deeper truths for our success as people and as leaders because it gives us proof that *we become what we think about.* This isn't some nice mantra or saying that has no real transformative power in our lives.

Here is my layman's version of epigenetics. *Epi* means "outer" and, of course, *genetics* refers to our genes. Scientists have proven that influences outside the genes and DNA themselves can influence the functioning of our genes and DNA. What we think about, whom we surround ourselves with, and the environment and energy we are exposed to can alter and change our DNA!

That's a very significant finding and one that can challenge many of our assumptions about our supposed predetermined destiny and our health and disease. Without doing a detailed analysis of what has transpired over the past 100-plus years about our DNA, here's a summary.

DNA (deoxyribonucleic acid) was first discovered and isolated by Friedrich Miescher in 1869. Fast forward to 1953 when two British gentlemen, James Watson and Francis Crick from Cambridge University (with help from many other scientists providing insight and previous work), determined the exact molecular structure and profiled the double helix we all have seen that represents what our DNA looks like. It is alleged that when Watson and Crick completed their work, they went to a local pub, and while hoisting a pint to celebrate said, "We've discovered the secret of life!"

From that point the race was on to unravel the secrets of life in a meaningful, scientific way. Fast forward to the year 2000 when two more men, Francis Collins and Craig Venter, stood with President Bill Clinton in the East Room of the White House and reported that for the very first time we could now read the genetic map and the coordinates of our DNA code. Thus the decoding of the human genome was accomplished.

This project took more than ten years and cost more than three billion dollars. They produced the details of the encoded message composed of over three billion "letters" of the four-letter genetic alphabet arranged in a well-defined sequence. That same effort can now be accomplished by a company called Illumina in about an hour for $100! The acceleration of knowledge and technology is best left to other authors, but it's great information for all of us to wrap our heads around and recognize another leadership truth—that we can no longer keep doing what we're doing; we must stay on the continual learner path.

When this project was first completed, most scientists in the field of microbiology and genetics believed that they could now predict with a high degree of accuracy exactly how a person's life would unfold regarding illnesses or diseases they would experience. But something happened on that road to discovering the secrets of life.

Within a few short years, microbiologists like Dr. Lipton made a stunning discovery. They believed, and were then able to prove in their labs, that a person's DNA is not fixed. Rather, it is affected by the "epi"—your attitude, your environment, the energy fields around you, and the people you are associated with, along with other factors.

One consequence of this is that many people have been healed or cured from their tragic accidents or diseases without the benefit of traditional medicines or therapy. One of the more successful and publicized of these is the story of Dr. Joe Dispenza. Dispenza was competing in a triathlon when he was struck by an SUV and sustained multiple bone fractures and severe damage to his spine.

He eschewed the advice of doctors who told him he would probably never walk again or if he did, he would have pain for the rest of his life no matter what they did. Dispenza decided to use the mind/body connection to manifest the healing in his body and spine. As he said, "What else was I going to do lying face down?"[3]

I also am very aware that there are many people who believe that Dispenza's story is too unbelievable to be real. What I know is he has been telling this story since it happened when he was 23, and he has the medical history to back up the fact that he was able to truly heal himself by his belief system. If you learn about the seriousness of his injuries and the fact that he has been able to lead a productive life without surgery to repair his badly damaged spine, I believe it would open your eyes to the power you hold in your mind by your beliefs.

If this new biology is true, then why can't we all activate it within our minds and bodies? Good question. In 2019 I gave a talk to a leadership group of about 75 people, and when it was over, one gentleman approached with a dire warning. "You need to be careful talking about this subject because it's not as simple as you make it sound." I thanked him for his comment and asked him to explain further. He floored me when he stated that he was a member of the Skeptics Society, and there was information that refuted Lipton and other scientists who subscribed to the new biology.

I looked at him and said, "There's such an organization?" He proudly said yes, that he was a member, and then gave me his and the Skeptics Society's reason for not embracing the idea and concept of epigenetics. If it were that simple—that our minds and what we believe about something could turn our DNA on or off, thereby eliminating disease—then why don't *all* people who reframe their belief systems and think themselves well automatically get cured?

It's a solid argument, and I'm not qualified to give a definitive answer. But there may be one possible answer. It potentially has to do with our conscious beliefs and our subconscious beliefs not being in alignment. Many of us have tried to rewrite our beliefs and change the course of our lives, and we have run into roadblocks. I'll cover that in more detail later in this section, but for now let me illustrate with several stories the power of the mind's ability to alter DNA and ultimately our reality.

A few years ago, my brother was diagnosed with stage four liver cancer. And as soon as he heard the diagnosis, he immediately said to the oncologist, "I do not want you to tell me how long you think I'm going to live." He continued, "Tell your entire team that no one is going to predict my lifespan. You tell me what the treatment protocol is, and we will do it, and we will keep going through it day by day. But let everybody on this team know that no one had better ever tell me how long they think I will live."

I don't know if you have ever had any experience with this disease within your circle of family or friends, but the typical life expectancy for stage four liver cancer is about six months. My brother lived for four and a half years. He recognized that the mere statement of an expected life span could produce that reality, and he wanted no part of it. He would not allow anyone to dictate his life span by telling him how long he was to live.

The reverse of that is the story of one of my former bosses. I arrived at the home office one day, and he wasn't there. I asked where he was and was told he had gone to the doctor. The next day we met at the office, and he told me the unfortunate news he had been given the day before, that he had glioblastoma brain cancer. The oncologist said that a person with the level of glioblastoma cancer he had in his brain typically lived 90 days. It saddens me to write this even now, so many years later, but he died *exactly 90 days* from the day his doctor stated these words: "The life expectancy for someone with glioblastoma such as yours is 90 days." It certainly seems that the doctor spoke reality into his being, and it manifested. If we ever needed proof that our words contain energy and power, this is a prime example.

One last story. I had a young executive who had previously worked for me receive the same diagnosis as my former boss—glioblastoma brain cancer. He refused to accept that he couldn't be healed, and he used his deep faith in God to drive his thinking in that manner. He did ultimately succumb to the cancer, but he lived another *two and a half years* of a mostly productive life and at one point was in complete and total remission.

You may ask why my brother and the former young executive weren't able to completely cure themselves. I am not a scientist or a doctor, so I don't have an exact answer, but both lived *far longer* than most people with their type of cancer. This suggests that the power of their beliefs enabled them to manifest a certain amount of healing in their bodies, which allowed them to live long past the life expectancy predicted by traditional medicine.

There you have three stories that exemplify this important point: What we think about, what we believe, what we put into our brains and focus on, and what we allow others to put into our brains can change our outcomes, sometimes in dramatic fashion. The biology of belief—that your mind contains power you may not realize—can be life altering. If ever there were a game-changer, I believe this is it.

How we are experiencing our day to day lives begs the question: How am I framing (believing) what is happening to me and my family, and how am I expressing that in my words and actions? To say that many of us live in stress mode is a huge understatement. What many have proven and what aligns with the biology of belief is that it's not stress that kills, but the way we frame and think about stress.

In an article published in the *Stanford News* in 2015 titled "Embracing Stress Is More Important than Reducing Stress," Clifton Barker outlined research conducted by Dr. Kelly McGonigal, author of the book *The Upside of Stress*, and assistant psychology professor Alia Crum. Barker stated that the three most *protective beliefs* about stress are: (1) to view your body's stress response as helpful, not debilitating; for example, to view stress as energy you can use; (2) to view yourself as able to handle, and even learn and grow from, the stress in your life; and (3) to view stress as something that everyone deals with, and not something that proves how uniquely screwed up you or your life is.[4]

Notice Barker's reference to "protective beliefs." This is a reference to how we use our beliefs to protect us from something we view as harmful. We'll explore this more later in this section, but for now recognize a powerful truth: *What you believe is foundational.* It can literally drive your destiny, as you'll discover in Chapter 4. As we move into exploring your own beliefs, I hope that you will embrace the ideas in the first chapter. Now let's take a look at other elements of belief systems.

POINTS TO REMEMBER

- Our beliefs can influence our physical bodies—even down to our DNA.
- You have the choice of what you believe and what information you allow in your mind—therefore, choose wisely what you believe!

CHAPTER 2

WHERE DO OUR BELIEFS ORIGINATE?

We learn our belief systems as very little children,
and then we move through life
creating experiences to match our beliefs.
Look back in your own life and notice how often
you have gone through the same experience.

—Louise Hay

The Covid situation challenged many of our long-held beliefs about medicine and science, whom to trust and whom not to trust. We each had to decide if we should take the advice from those considered authorities, such as primary care doctors and government leaders, or do we take personal control of our health and our decisions and possibly make different choices? Your choice likely follows the path of your established beliefs (and biases!) that previously rose from personal experience. We could be like my parents and in-laws in that whatever the doctor said, they did without question. But when the doctor told my dad that they would probably have to cut off his leg just below his knee due a wound that wouldn't heal due to his diabetes, even my dad found an alternative treatment. The bad outcome motivated him to challenge his long-held beliefs about what to do. He took control of his own decisions and saved his leg from amputation.

My goal with this section is not to convince you of what your choices should be. It's rather to point out the obvious: What you do is driven by your established beliefs, which include your biases about all the related things, especially when it comes to big decisions.

Here's a personal story to illustrate the origins of our beliefs. I grew up in a very dysfunctional home. The early years of my life created in my brain a near-constant fight or flight mode, and that did not allow my brain to develop healthy attachments or to feel secure. I'm also convinced that the lack of attachments, bonding, and healthy love showed up as ADD. And I believe that it created other issues for me as well that have taken a lifetime to unravel.

One of my early childhood experiences shaped a core belief in me that has been destructive, and it has been one of the major obstacles I've had to overcome. It is painful to admit and write about.

My mother, for some reason, believed that she was being a good parent by letting me quit things. An early example is when I came home from preschool the day we had been taught how to tie our shoes. I couldn't learn how to do it. I don't remember exactly what happened at school that day, but I believe there was some teasing, and I felt frustrated and embarrassed. Whatever method the teachers were using did not work for me. I cried at school and was still crying when my mother picked me up. What would a healthy mother/son relationship look like at that moment? She would have helped me at home until I accomplished the task there. And even if I couldn't, she would have encouraged me to go back to school the next day and keep trying no matter what. But she didn't. I never went back to preschool.

She let me quit because I failed the first time I tried to learn something new at a very critical age. A few years later, I attended a couple of Cub Scout meetings, but for some reason that I don't remember I came home and told her I didn't want to go back. Again, she let me quit.

Think about the imprint of letting me quit when things got tough or if I just didn't like them. My brain was building a strong connection between trying something, failing, then feeling frustrated, inadequate, or embarrassed, and then easily quitting. In brain science neurons that fire together wire together.

Many times, my mother thought she was protecting me by letting me quit, but in the end, she was causing tremendous harm as this pattern began to manifest in beliefs throughout my life. It has taken a lifetime to unravel the neural pathways in my brain that were created by those events I was allowed to quit.

Think about the incredibly huge, core belief I developed—*I am a quitter!* I'm almost in tears as I write this because it conjures up so many memories of being defeated and walking away when I could have and should have stayed the course. It would have saved me much anguish if I had and developed new neural pathways earlier in my life that would have built up a stronger self-perception and self-esteem and therefore stronger beliefs about who I am and what I am capable of.

Have I overcome that early learning? Yes, in most cases, but it is still a potential source of the imposter syndrome for me that I must be vigilant to recognize and then follow strategies to silence that voice and keep moving forward.

I want you to understand how powerful the embedded scripts and beliefs are that we each have and potentially where they may have come from. They are literally either the roadblock to your dreams and goals or the catalyst to achieving anything that you want to achieve. Yet I've found that most people don't know what their scripts or beliefs are or what needs to be changed.

You may have seen glimpses of yourself in my stories. Maybe yours are more dramatic or maybe they aren't, but the point is that we all have beliefs, they've been building inside us all our lives in many ways, and they are the foundation to pursuing and achieving our goals and dreams—or to hindering them.

Your beliefs are the essence of your being. Recognize that what you believe is true—whether it is or isn't!

"Whether you believe you can or you believe you can't, you're right!" Most people attribute that statement to Henry Ford, but evidence suggests that the quote preceded him, and some have even attributed it to Confucius, but whoever said it, it's a powerful message that deserves our attention and examination. The mere difference of "I can't do this," versus "I can't do this…yet," could be the difference between a life of fulfillment and goal achievement or a life of frustration and quitting before you start. *What we say to ourselves about ourselves, and our potential, contains power that you and I might not be able to fully comprehend.*

Albert Einstein said, "Reality is an illusion, albeit a very persistent one." Was he saying there is no such thing as reality as we know it? I believe that he was and would suggest that you embrace that belief as well so that you can unlock a new future for you and the people that you are leading now or in the future. Even if you lead no one else other than yourself at this point, wouldn't you rather have the view that all things are possible versus putting a governor on your engine of creativity and achievement? If there truly is no such thing as reality, then why not create the reality that you want?

As it relates to leadership, this is where we find ourselves today. It's important to step back and deeply examine where our beliefs came from and whether they are channeling us to achieve our version of success and our dreams and goals. We arrive in any given situation with beliefs about ourselves that have been forming inside of our minds since the day we were born and maybe even when we were in the womb. Our parents, teachers, friends, environment, and many other circumstances largely form what we believe about ourselves, others, and the world around us. Internal forces, such as our intuition and emotions, drive us to determine a belief. And external forces, driven primarily by authority figures, experiences, logic, and science, also cause us to form beliefs.

The beliefs we have are powerful, in potentially both negative and positive manners. And they act as a compass, at times determining our decisions and ultimately the direction of our lives. They can control us without us realizing that we can be trapped in a twisted mind game of moving back and forth between two completely opposed realities of who we think we are and who we really are—and more profoundly, who we can become. We'll explore that idea more in the next chapter when we look at the conscious and subconscious minds.

What I've discovered over 13 years of executive and leadership coaching is that very few people take the time to examine their beliefs beyond a superficial level. Beliefs act as an incredible compass, and examining them is foundational and essential to uncovering whether what we believe is empowering us toward our dreams and goals or holding us back.

When we think about our beliefs and recognize that our brains are trying to make sense of the world around us, we must also realize that our brains will *lie* to us as they view events and circumstances. That may come as a shock—that your brain will lie to you—but it's the truth. As Einstein alluded, your brain doesn't know fact from fiction, and it's constantly trying to make sense of things you're experiencing in a way that protects you and keeps you safe.

Maybe you've seen the National Geographic show *Brain Games*. If you have, then you know exactly what I'm talking about. If not, you can probably find it on one of the streaming services. I highly recommend it if you want to understand this concept at a deeper level. The show provides real-life examples of how your brain will misinterpret what it's experiencing and seeing, thereby completely distorting reality and potentially creating false beliefs that keep you from pursuing and achieving your goals and dreams.

When we try to do this thing called personal leadership, leading others and building relationships, we have fits and starts because we may have arrived with a belief system that isn't aligned with where we want to go. If you don't believe in yourself then why should others?

In Chapter 5 of this section, we'll dive deeper into the beliefs that you have and explore a method to reframe our beliefs. For now, just understand that many of the beliefs you're carrying are not yours. You've inherited them from all that you've experienced in your life, and they are running your life in ways you probably don't realize.

At one point most people on the planet believed that the Earth was flat. In the nineteenth century an English writer named Samuel Rowbotham continued to espouse this belief and wrote a book called *Earth Not a Globe*.[1] Even today you can join The Flat Earth Society. When you realize that ancient Greek philosophy believed Earth was spherical and that Plato wrote about a spherical Earth in the fourth century BC, it's easier to understand how we mere mortals can have faulty belief systems.

And we have all seen this play out with the New Reality we've entered. We're surrounded by so many different opinions and beliefs that it's hard to know what is true or not true. We've had to figure out what to believe based on our trusted sources.

An example is that during Covid, a friend told me that natural antibody immunity lasted only two months. I told her I believed that wasn't true, that the research I'd read said it could be up to a year, and new research investigating bone marrow showed that a person who had Covid might have lifetime immunity, but it was still too early to make any emphatic statement. I also had relatives who still had the antibodies a full year after their Covid diagnosis.

The point is to examine where you're getting your information, how it's affecting your belief systems, and then realize how your biases affect what you believe. Especially the bias called *confirmation bias*. A deep discussion on that topic is beyond the intent of this book, but for our purposes here, recognize how your mindset and what you choose to believe affects what you're willing to explore, learn, and decide.

Many times in the coaching work I do, and especially at the International Institute for Management Development in the High Performance Leadership program I coached in for almost a decade, I would look at a particular person and say, "If only you could see yourself the way I am seeing you. You have power you don't even know that you have, and it's just waiting for you to acknowledge it, believe it, accept it, and use it!" Often other people in the group would immediately leap on the comment and say that they've sensed the same thing about this person, and that the person held back and did not lean into their own personal power.

This is what is called the *person effect*, which I'll cover more in the third section. Each of us in the group felt, sensed, and saw how powerful this person innately was, and yet they themselves hadn't embraced it!

How could we explain this in another way? There is another possibility, which I referenced in the earlier story of developing the habit of quitting. And I've confirmed this by working with many leaders. It's called *imposter syndrome*. One of the authorities on the subject is Clare Josa, who in her 2020 landmark book, *Ditching Imposter Syndrome,* validated its existence and its cost to each of us and to the companies we work in.[2] This syndrome is much more than just a lack of confidence.

The idea of the term *impostor phenomenon* was first introduced by Dr. Pauline R. Clance and Dr. Suzanne A. Imes in a 1978 article titled "The Impostor Phenomenon in High Achieving Women: Dynamics and Therapeutic Intervention."[3] Clance and Imes describe the imposter phenomenon as when people who have status, achievements, and recognition of their worth or who they are, yet deep inside their heart and mind they think of themselves as being unworthy, fake, or an imposter.

They interviewed 150 high-achieving women in the United States who had earned degrees, high test scores, and formal recognition of their professional excellence and achievements. Despite all this external validation, internally these women could not acknowledge their own accomplishments. They explained their success as resulting from luck or that other people simply overestimated their intelligence and abilities. Clance and Imes hold that this mindset develops out of factors like gender stereotypes, early family dynamics, and culture. They also note that these women exhibited symptoms of depression, anxiety, and low self-confidence.

Based on their clinical experience, Clance and Imes state that the impostor phenomenon is less prevalent in men. But Josa's research provides a more comprehensive and updated view and finds that 49 percent of men also deal with this syndrome versus 52 percent of women.

On a coaching call with a client, whom I'll call Sue, based on what I was hearing, I posed the question, "Do you think you are dealing with a lack of confidence? Or is it the impostor syndrome?" After we discussed the difference, Sue thought for a moment and said it was probably the latter, and that the main driver of her impostor syndrome was that she had never finished college. This thinking held her back. I pointed out to her my track record and asked if she thought my bio was impressive. She said it was. I then told her that I too had never graduated from college. Something in my intuition told me to add one more piece of data—that I had thought about lying on my resume a few times early in my career but that I had resisted and stayed true to my values and integrity even though it was hard when I knew I had been passed over for jobs because of it.

Sue was surprised and thankful to hear this because her sister had recently suggested that she lie on her resume. That is how insidious the impostor syndrome can be for people.

I probed a bit further and asked if, beyond her not graduating from college, she had any understanding of why she held such a deep-seated belief that she was an imposter. Without going into detail, she said that she'd had a very tough life and experienced a lot of traumas.

Most of us know that people who have experienced trauma in their early developmental years can experience shame and guilt because their brain places the blame on themselves, and they're not sure how to correct the faulty belief that they weren't at fault. And this can lead to deep-seated beliefs about being an impostor or not being worthy of achieving success, even after achieving it. Since I am an executive coach and not a therapist, we didn't take a deep dive into what Sue had experienced, and I honored the code that we International Coach Federation certified coaches adhere to and provided a referral to a therapist in her area.

In wrapping up this chapter, here's a question for you to consider: Do you really know what your beliefs are, and do you know where they came from? If you can answer both of those questions, then the next question to answer is this: What beliefs are holding you back and should be rewritten, and what beliefs are positive and powerful and should be leveraged even more?

This leads us to the next chapter to examine what we think we believe about ourselves versus what is actually true.

POINTS TO REMEMBER

- Our beliefs, many of which we inherit, are powerful and guide us like a compass in both negative and positive ways.
- You may have power you don't even know you have, waiting for you to acknowledge it.
- If you have high achievements but inside you feel unworthy or fake, you may be carrying the impostor syndrome.

CHAPTER 3

THE BATTLE BETWEEN OUR CONSCIOUS AND SUBCONSCIOUS MINDS

Until you make the unconscious conscious,
it will control your life and you will call it fate.

—Carl Jung

If you think about the scenario I described in the previous chapter with Sue, that she had suffered traumas and a tough life and therefore possibly developed the belief that she was somehow at fault, then we understand how we can hold a belief that is real to *us* but is *not reality*. I don't know what kind of traumas Sue experienced, but more than likely, especially if they happened when she was a child, she wasn't at fault. She could have been a victim of the dysfunctional family or system that she grew up in.

This dilemma of the battle between our conscious and subconscious minds explains why it is sometimes extremely hard to change what we believe, what we think, and how we act. We set conscious goals for ourselves that we don't achieve because our subconscious mind may not believe that we deserve to achieve that goal. In *Triggers: Creating Behavior That Lasts—Becoming the Person You Want to Be,* Marshall Goldsmith describes this conundrum as the conflict between the planner and the doer.[1] We plan and set goals, then fail to act on them to achieve them. His antidote is accountability. Since I am an executive coach, this suggestion aligns with the work I've done over the past 13 years and the success my clients have had by introducing a coach into their growth and development, and more importantly, reframing their beliefs. But the additional information of understanding this battle between our conscious and subconscious explains why we might need accountability in the first place!

Sigmund Freud posited the theory that we have three levels of awareness: (1) conscious, (2) preconscious, and (3) unconscious (which I'll call subconscious). Preconscious thoughts are those that we aren't thinking of at the moment, but we can think of easily if we choose to or if something triggers us to think about them. That is, we're not thinking these thoughts right now, but we can easily do so. As Julia Thomas puts it in her article "What Is the Preconscious and What Does It Mean to Me?" in *Better Help*: "This interpretation of Freudian theory makes a clear distinction between the part of the mind we can access and the part we can't. However, whether the preconscious mind is a part of the unconscious or not, all three aspects of the mind can work together as we perceive and make decisions about our beliefs and our life."[2]

Our conscious mind is where we perceive our own reality and experience of the world and everything around us. It's where we judge, think, and make decisions. And it is most active when we are awake. There has been a lot of debate for the past 100 years about the unconscious mind versus the subconscious mind, but for the sake of this book, I will use the term subconscious mind simply because the definition of unconscious means we aren't awake and therefore are not able to activate it.

The subconscious mind is where we have stored a lifetime of events, memories, and experiences. And this is where we have formed our beliefs and judgments of those events. Most importantly, it's where our self image and self beliefs are established.

One expert on changing our beliefs is Marisa Peer, author, therapist, and hypnotherapist trainer. In a TEDx event about the mind, she said that, (1) "Your mind does exactly what it thinks is in your best interest."

(2) "Your mind is hard-wired to move toward pleasure and away from pain." (3) "Your mind constructs the way you feel about things all the time, and it boils it down to two things, (a) the pictures you have in your head, and (b) the words you say to yourself." And (4) "Your mind loves what is familiar and is programmed to move toward what is familiar." For change to happen and to change your beliefs, you have to reverse this— *"Make what is unfamiliar familiar and vice versa as well as speak pleasure into what is otherwise painful which tells our brain that we enjoy the pain because of what we will gain from it."*[3]

Another way to say what Peer is suggesting, which I use many times in my executive coaching, is that we must become comfortable being uncomfortable in order to move beyond our current beliefs and achieve the goals we want to achieve. When we are stretching, growing, and trying new things, it can be very uncomfortable for a time, but we must persevere and keep moving forward in order for new beliefs, habits, and skills to accumulate.

Examples of this idea come from two famous people, Arnold Schwarzenegger and Muhammad Ali. Schwarzenegger says this about what he believes drove his success: "Modesty isn't a word that applies to me, and it never will."[4] He never feared being successful, nor did he apologize for his bravado. The same goes for Ali. He believed that fear stops most people from taking on challenges, and he told himself that he was the greatest long before he actually achieved greatness in his sport. I vividly remember seeing him on TV as he was coming onto the boxing scene and Howard Cosell interviewed him. His positivity absolutely screamed through his proclamation, "I am the greatest!"

Both examples amplify the point that if we don't believe in ourselves and our abilities, then why would anyone else believe in us? And they are extreme examples of people harnessing the power of the conscious mind to formulate words and statements that drive the imprint of their beliefs deep into their subconscious. Did Schwarzenegger and Ali have self-doubt at times? I don't know, but when you look at their careers, their beliefs, words, and actions manifested the success they each achieved. My parents' reaction to Ali wasn't very positive because they had the belief that you shouldn't boast and brag about yourself. They believed that you should be humble. Did that belief stick with me? Yes, it did for a very long time in a way that held me back. I believe that I am still very humble today, but I no longer have a problem identifying my successes and accomplishments in a positive way.

I referenced Dispenza's natural healing from traumatic spinal injuries. In his story is a vivid picture of what harnessing the conscious and subconscious minds looks like. His training in chiropractic care had alerted him to the fact that this incredible body and brain we are born with contains an ability to heal itself.

He says, "First, every day I would put all of my conscious attention on this intelligence within me and give it a plan, a template, a vision, with very specific orders, and then I would surrender my healing to this greater mind that has unlimited power, allowing it to do the healing for me. And second, I wouldn't let any thought slip by my awareness that I didn't want to experience."[5]

He had to become "aware of his awareness" to eliminate the subconscious mind from interfering with the healing he was manifesting with his conscious mind. You will notice in Dispenza's quote the intentional effort he undertakes to eliminate that disconnect between his conscious and subconscious mind.

Here's a graphic that helps us understand the conscious and subconscious mind and how they actually work against each other.

Conscious Mind vs Subconscious Mind

CONSCIOUS MIND

The Conscious Mind tries to use willpower to control behaviours, habits and beliefs but loses out to the Subconscious Mind's greater influence.

- Critical Thinking
- Logical Thinking
- Short term Memory
- Willpower

SUBCONSCIOUS MIND

Since it is not conscious and incapable of reasoning is therefore non judgemental and is very flexible and one could think of it as the hard drive of the brain constantly being programmed with life's data.

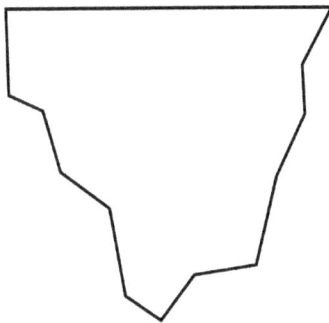

- Beliefs
- Creativity
- Development Stages
- Emotions & Feelings
- Habits & addictions
- Imagination
- Intuition
- Long term memory
- Values

POINTS TO REMEMBER

- You may not be achieving your goals because your conscious mind conflicts with your subconscious mind.
- We must become comfortable being uncomfortable to move beyond our current beliefs and achieve the goals we want to achieve.
- Tell and repeat to yourself what you want your subconscious mind to believe.

CHAPTER 4

WHAT DO YOU BELIEVE ABOUT YOU?

Your beliefs become your thoughts,
your thoughts become your words,
your words become your actions,
your actions become your habits,
your habits become your values,
and your values become your destiny.

—Mahatma Gandhi

1st **Self Awareness**

5th
Lead Others
and Ourselves

Ed Chaffin
UnCommon Leadership®

2nd
Self Management

4th
Manage
Relations

3rd
Other
Awareness

The UnCommon Leadership® Model

One more time for emphasis: If you don't believe in yourself as a leader, then why would anyone else believe in you? As leaders, we must portray confidence and belief in our knowledge, skills, and competencies if we are to be able to lead others effectively. It is truly the starting point for understanding the foundation for great leaders and for greater leadership.

Gandhi's quote is great because of its simple yet undeniable truth: Our destiny is defined by the foundational beliefs that we hold.

And combined with the awareness that our beliefs drive our destiny, as in Figure 1 of the UnCommon Leadership® model, we recognize that leadership begins with our self-awareness and self-management or personal leadership. Personal leadership is the foundation upon which all other forms and methods for leading rely. We must have an accurate self-assessment of who we are as leaders.

We'll explore later the best way to accomplish that in Chapter 18. For now, please understand how important this is because it is my belief that most of us have only some vague ideas of who we are as leaders and how we affect others.

Leading yourself requires a deeper understanding of who you are, what drives you, and what your natural, default leadership styles are. It starts and it ends with you having an accurate view of exactly who you are as a leader. As I referenced in regards to how your beliefs are formed, I firmly believe that who you are determines how you lead. And who you are is the sum of everything that has happened to you since the day you were born (and possibly even while you were in the womb).

What has happened in your life manifests in you through your beliefs. The things you experience through life form the belief systems and ideas you hold about yourself, others, and the world. Some of those beliefs do not empower us toward our goals and dreams. Some aren't even ours. They were put there by well-meaning adults or authority figures, and we either consciously or subconsciously adopted them.

Let me add one more important concept around the idea that your destiny begins with your beliefs. Before we explore your personal beliefs, let's look at one more emphatic quote that amplifies just how powerful our beliefs are. This frequently used quote comes from Earl Nightingale: "You are now, and you do become, what you think about."[1]

He is considered the father of the "motivational tape" and was the founder of Nightingale Conant in 1960 alongside Lloyd Conant. That organization took the self-development idea to an entirely new level. I have no idea how many tape sets I ordered from them during my own personal transformative years, but it was a lot.

Nightingale was one of only twelve Marines who survived the 1941 Japanese attack on the battleship Arizona in Pearl Harbor. After the war, he went into the radio broadcast business and started a radio program called *Our Changing World* on the radio station WGN in Chicago. He produced the spoken word record, *The Strangest Secret* in 1956, and it became the first one of its kind to achieve Gold Record status, acquiring million-seller status.

And what is the strangest secret? We become what we think about. And, he often added, "Most of the time!"

If we put these two quotes together—our beliefs become our destiny, and we become what we think about—we begin to realize the power of our brain and our beliefs, what we say about ourselves, and what we focus on.

For some, this combination is called the Law of Attraction, which is what Napoleon Hill wrote about in his book *Think and Grow Rich,* which had a profound effect on Earl Nightingale. If you want a better life, if you want success, however you define success for yourself, then *think* your way to that goal! It's as simple as that, right? If it is, then why don't so many of us achieve what we set out to achieve?

It's an easy question to ask, but the answer is complex because we are dealing with a complex organ, the brain. As we saw in the previous chapter, one of the major reasons is the disconnect between our conscious and subconscious minds. The exploration of our brains, though, is rapidly evolving, and every year we learn more and more about the complexities and wonders of our brains. The field of brain-based leadership is set up for an explosion over the next 20 years and is being led by organizations like the Academy of Brain-based Leadership (ABL), located in

California, from which I have a certificate in brain-based leadership, and the NeuroLeadership Institute in Asolo, Italy.

I am confident there will be a time when we look back in amazement that we were trying to do this leadership thing without a deep understanding of our very own brain first!

Let's examine some of the beliefs that we may have. As a prelude, ponder this quote from James E. Alcock:

> Our thoughts and feelings, our actions and reactions, respond not to the world as it actually is—for we never know reality directly—but to the world as we believe it to be. Because of our beliefs, we brush our teeth or don't bother; we vote for Jennifer and not for John; we eat certain foods and avoid others; we worship one deity or another or none at all, and we rely on scientific medicine or homeopathy to cure our ills.[2]

Here's a brief list of both positive and negative beliefs. As you read them, consider if any of them resonate with who you perceive yourself to be.

Positive beliefs we may carry:

- All things are possible.
- If it's to be, it's up to me.
- People are basically good at heart.
- If I believe it, then I can achieve it.
- I am in charge of my life.
- If I work hard, I'll be successful.
- I am worthy of _____.
- There is opportunity around every corner.

- Failure is good because I learn from it each time.
- My past can be reviewed and rewritten.
- Stress can be a positive motivator.

Negative beliefs we may carry:

- I don't deserve to be happy.
- I am a bad person.
- I am not good enough.
- I don't have enough education.
- Stress will kill you.
- You can't count on others to do what needs to be done.
- People will let you down.
- I am a slow learner.
- I deserve to be miserable.
- I am a quitter.
- The world isn't fair.
- People are basically evil.
- No good deed goes unpunished!

This list could be endless on both positive and negative beliefs, but you get the idea. My encouragement at the end of this section will be to take some focused time to examine your belief systems and especially those core beliefs we'll look at in the next chapter.

It might surprise you to discover what you actually believe, both positive and negative. But it can be the secret—just like The Strangest Secret—to unlocking your true potential as a person and as a leader.

Realize how important it may be for you to think deeply and put on paper the beliefs that will empower you so that you can leverage them. And do the same for your limiting beliefs as you'll see in the instructions below for this chapter. Enjoy the process. Remember, it's a belief to choose to enjoy it!

POINTS TO REMEMBER

- If you don't believe in yourself as a leader, then why would anyone else believe in you?
- Our destiny is defined by the foundational beliefs we hold.
- Who you are determines how you lead. And who you are is the sum of everything that has happened to you since the day you were born.
- We become what we think about.

ACTION ITEMS

1. Think about and examine your beliefs.
2. Make a list of your positive beliefs and then rewrite them in this form:
   a. I am convinced that all things are possible.
   b. I am able to achieve what I set out to achieve.
   c. I am worthy of the successes that I experience.
3. Make a list of your beliefs that may be holding you back from achieving your goals and dreams. Then rewrite them to be powerful statements.
   d. "I don't deserve to be happy," becomes, "I choose to be happy in this moment."
   e. "I am a quitter," becomes, "I am resilient, and I finish what I start."
   f. "People will let you down," becomes, "I expect people to deliver what they promise."

CHAPTER 5

REWIRING OUR BRAINS FOR NEW BELIEFS

Because of the power of neuroplasticity,
you can, in fact, reframe your world and
rewire your brain so that you are more objective.
You have the power to see things as they are
so that you can respond thoughtfully, deliberately,
and effectively to everything that you experience.

—Elizabeth Thornton

Now that we've covered some of the positive and negative beliefs that we may hold on to, let's examine how we can rewire our brains to create new neural pathways that can produce tremendous growth. I'll start with a story to underscore how I was able to rewire my brain for a new belief system that lifted me out of the belief that "I am a quitter." This story is an example of the fact that our beliefs can be changed, and sometimes it's not that hard.

If I asked you, "How would you like to improve your performance by almost 20 percent, and the only thing that you have to do is change your focus and your beliefs?" What would your answer be? I believe that virtually 100 percent of the population would take me up on the offer.

"Ed, the only thing I must do is change what I focus on and change what I believe, and I'll achieve a 20 percent improvement in what I'm doing? I don't have to train harder, sign up for a course, or totally reinvent who I am? Sign me up!"

I experienced this a few years ago when I was a competitive cyclist. I wasn't at the Tour de France professional level, but I was a fairly good rider. I rode with a bike club in Tempe, Arizona that was led by a former Italian pro racer named Dominic. At the time I was a Category 4 racer. But there were only 4 categories, so I didn't have to do much to gain that classification other than compete in a few races.

While living in the Phoenix area and riding for Dominic's team, I got to know and help one of my cycling idols, Michael Secrest, raise funds to do an epic ride around the Phoenix Motor Speedway, where he was attempting to break the record for the most miles ridden over 24 hours. Michael had also competed in, and several times won, the RAAM (the Race Across America), an epic, brutal, race from the west coast to the east coast of the US. I became a huge fan of his. The event that radically altered my view of what is possible for myself, which in turn changed my beliefs, happened in a 100-kilometer bike race south of Phoenix.

Michael was the guest celebrity racer for the race that day, and it started in Casa Grande, Arizona. The race was about to kick off, and I wrestled my way to the front of the pack to greet him. Once we exchanged hellos, I turned my attention to my feedback mechanism, the cyclometer on my handlebars, to make sure it was set to zero and was tracking my front wheel. But something was wrong and no matter what I did, the cyclometer wouldn't work. I was frustrated beyond description. Then the starter announced through his megaphone that the race was about to start.

At that moment, I realized that I had to give up the effort to get the cyclometer to work and focus on the race. In every race that I previously did, my cyclometer had been the feedback mechanism that told me how fast I was going and if I was on track with my capabilities—which equated to my beliefs about what I thought I could accomplish.

But in this crisis of a broken cyclometer, something had to change. So, I made a vow: *I will stay with Michael and the lead pack as long as I can.* That was the change in my focus.

As the race commenced, I had no feedback. I had no idea how fast I was going. No idea of the RPMs my pedaling was producing. No idea even how far we had gone to know how much longer I could keep going at my exertion level. Nothing at all to know how I was doing except measuring my progress by my original focus and goal—finishing with the lead pack and staying on the back wheel of my idol as long as I could.

Before this race, my personal best in a 100-mile race was four hours and 38 minutes, which is an average speed of 23.5 mph. Not bad but not pro category—not even Category 1 pace. I had believed that was the best I could do unless I changed my training or trained harder. That thinking and belief had driven my focus and efforts.

As the current race unfolded, the first part contained a lot of hills and climbing. It was a monumental struggle to stay with the lead pack. Fortunately, about halfway through the race, we found fairly flat roads, and it became a bit easier to stay with the lead pack even though several times I started dropping off and had to make a herculean effort to dig deep within and see if I had anything left in the tank to get back to the back of the lead pack.

I had no idea how many miles we had ridden, how many were remaining, or how fast I was going. The only thing I had was the motivation and desire to stay with Michael and the lead pack. Just when I thought that I couldn't maintain the pace of the lead group any longer, someone shouted, "Right turn ahead." With that pronouncement, the lead pack slowed down to make the 90-degree turn, and once we all cleared the turn, the finish line was in sight, and the sprinters dropped the hammer and pulled way ahead.

I was dropped like a lead balloon! But if you know anything about cycling you would know that as long as I didn't drop too far off the back of the pack, I would receive the same time as the main peloton group. I crossed the finish line and rode over to someone who I knew was checking his cyclometer and asked him what our average speed had been for the finish time of two hours and 22 minutes that was displayed on the huge timing mechanism stretched across the road.

His answer shocked me: 27.5 mph. I had just ridden 62 miles at an average pace of 27.5 mph! That was four miles per hour faster than I had ever ridden any distance of over 50 miles. I was stunned. The net increase was a 17 percent improvement with no additional training.

All I did was refocus on a new goal with no feedback about how I was doing other than my dedication to staying with the lead pack. More importantly, I didn't quit on my original commitment. The epiphany was that I realized just how much my previous focus and beliefs had been holding me back from being a better rider.

The lesson I learned from that event was to stop training with a cyclometer and just go out and push myself until I couldn't go any further. This brought a huge shift in my ability to be a better teammate to the other cyclists.

As a cyclist, I was literally turned loose that day because I realized how much my own beliefs about what I could achieve had been distorted by my confirmation biases!

This personal story illustrates that it is possible to reframe and rewrite our beliefs and at times, we can even do it "in the moment." When necessary, changing my belief was fairly easy. The effort that followed wasn't easy, but the catalyst for the change was easy. I simply set a goal that hitherto I believed was impossible—and I didn't quit. This event was also the catalyst for a Disney Marathon I ran 14 years later when I had pulled my groin muscle three weeks before the race. I managed to complete the marathon because years earlier I had generated new belief systems about what was possible by reframing my situation and goals. Was it easy to complete that marathon? Absolutely not. It was awful! But I did it based on the foundational beliefs I had established in that bike race.

There was one more factor, though, in driving me to even attempt to run, much less complete, that marathon, and I'll address this in the last chapter of this section—accountability. I referenced this earlier as a key factor in our growth and development. I had committed to my daughter Stacy to run the marathon with her, and I didn't want to let her down. She finished more than two hours ahead of me, but when I walked up to her while she was laying on the ground resting, and she saw the Mickey Mouse medallion around my neck signifying that I had completed the Disney Marathon, the feeling of exhilaration overwhelmed me to see how proud she was of me. That's the power of someone alongside you for making the changes you want to make.

In examining our beliefs and deciding what we would like to change, I can't emphasize that the exercise of doing just that—challenging your beliefs—may be the most important undertaking you've ever attempted. No matter where you are in your life, or whether you've examined your beliefs or not, I encourage you to embrace this idea and the suggestions that I am providing. If you do, then the rest of the book will have an even greater impact on you, your self-leadership, and the leader that you become.

One of the best resources and authorities I've discovered for examining our thoughts, and therefore our beliefs, is Gary van Warmerdam's book, *Mindworks: A Practical Guide for Changing Thoughts, Beliefs, and Emotional Reactions*. I also recommend that you view YouTube videos he has produced. Here is a quote from *Mindworks*: "Reacting emotionally is made instantly, emotionally, and silently within the belief system. Beliefs are like preset programs in the mind that launch emotional reactions when activated."[1]

Van Warmerdam indicates that the most important beliefs to examine are our core beliefs because they are the drivers and the source for the extended beliefs that regularly manifest. Our core beliefs drive our emotional reactions, which build up connections in our brain as events occur in our life. Those emotional reactions produce our thoughts, behavioral responses, and our negative thinking, which can create our automatic reactions when we are triggered. It's necessary to examine the full spectrum of our belief system that we have developed, starting with our core beliefs.

What are core beliefs? Gary provides an example in one of his YouTube videos.[2] Some of us may be driven by the thought, *I have to be right*. That thought drives behaviors like one-upping others, arguing, and making it unpleasant for others to be around us. The thought that *I have to be right* hides the fact that our core beliefs may be more insidious, such as, "If I'm not right, then I'm stupid," "I'm worthless," or "I'm a failure." These core beliefs create the emotions we experience such as pride, fear, or anger. When we understand how powerful these emotions are, we can then realize how challenging it is to change our beliefs because at times we are emotional animals!

We must be able to step back and view our beliefs and identities with a new lens—that of the skeptic who is willing to challenge long-held beliefs and become a neutral observer. We have convictions and certainties about our beliefs, and these must be challenged. In doing so, we examine our faith. Van Warmerdam speaks here of faith not in the religious sense, but the faith that your belief is accurate about yourself.

That faith has driven your conviction, and that conviction is what needs to be examined in order to change your beliefs by creating new, positive convictions about your core beliefs.

I highly recommend Gary's videos for a start and then his book, *Mindworks*, for a more in-depth description. I've done a lot of research, and I believe he has some of the best, actionable information that has been written about changing our beliefs.

Once we have examined our core beliefs and have been convinced of the need to change them—as we've realized how much they hold us back from being all that we can be—how do we begin to rewrite them? One of the ways that I have been able to rewrite the beliefs and scripts that have held me back is to rewire my brain using repetitive mantras. I learned this many years ago, and it has helped me to create greater neural pathways in my brain that can interrupt the negative patterns created in my earlier life. Remember, neurons that fire together wire together, and it's this rewiring that can completely alter who you are and where you're going.

In the early 1900s, a man named Emile Coue introduced this concept, and he said that by saying positive affirmations to yourself in the mirror, you can start to reprogram your brain into a different reality. This is because your subconscious is like the base of your mind that lies covered by your active consciousness. As we've discussed before, the two don't always match up. And you may find it hard to change your core beliefs if you don't regularly practice changing subconscious thought patterns. The key is consistency. Do this every day until you cut through and affect your mind at its very core.

If you think about the old vinyl records that we used to play on our record players, they had grooves on the record that, when the needle ran over them, played sounds. They were destined to play the same sound every time the needle ran over the record.

But if you were to scratch the record enough, the needle couldn't play the sounds any longer. The analogy is a bit off in that you can't rewrite the grooves of a record; you can only disrupt them to stop them from playing what had been recorded. Fortunately, our brains are much better than vinyl records because they can be rewritten to play different music. It's called *neuroplasticity*, and what we know is that no matter your age, you can rewrite the grooves in your brain, learn new things, and create new neural pathways for growth.

This is the first step in rewriting our beliefs and scripts: Identify what "groove" needs to be halted in its tracks, and then create the mantra or mantras to rewrite the track in our brain.

Our brains can be "rewired," creating new neurons and new neural connections, or pathways, if we decide to articulate a different version of ourselves that drives us toward our goals and dreams.

Let's use my early childhood core belief of "I am a quitter" as an example. I referenced several beliefs that resulted from that early experience of my mother letting me quit so easily, and those were secondary beliefs that showed up as the Imposter Syndrome.

How have I overcome that core belief? One of the first and most powerful ways I accomplished this was to write down several positive statements on a three-by-five card and keep it in my Day-Timer. I continued to read them every day for about two years.

Where did the idea for this come from? As I was on the reinvention path, several books had a dramatic influence on me, and Og Mandino's book *The Greatest Salesman in the World* was one of the first. That is where I got the three-by-five card idea.

From his book here are the ten scrolls (or mantras, to use the term I referenced earlier):

1. Today I begin a new life.
2. I will greet this day with love in my heart.
3. I will persist until I succeed.
4. I am God's greatest miracle.
5. I will live this day as if it is my last.
6. Today I will be master of my emotions.
7. I will laugh at the world.
8. Today I will multiply my value a hundredfold
9. I will act now.
10. I will pray for guidance.

In Mandino's fable the protagonist uses the scrolls, or mantras, this way:

I will read each scroll for thirty days in this prescribed manner before I proceed to the next scroll.

First, I will read the words in silence when I arise. Then, I will read the words in silence after I have partaken of my mid-day meal. Last, I will read the words again just before I retire at day's end, and most importantly, on this occasion, I will read the words aloud.

On the next day, I will repeat this procedure, and I will continue in like manner for thirty days. Then, I will turn to the next scroll and repeat this procedure for another thirty days. I will continue in this manner until I have lived with each scroll for thirty days and my reading has become a habit.[3]

I didn't do it exactly as it was prescribed in the book, but I did it, and it completely rewired my brain and ultimately eliminated many self-destructive beliefs, especially the core belief that I was a quitter. That allowed me to have the two experiences I've described—the bike race and the marathon, as well as the complete reinvention of my career after retiring in 2008. I am convinced that had I not begun the rewiring process, I would have never attempted to become a competitive cyclist, much less ride at the speed and level I accomplished, nor would I have run a marathon with a pulled groin muscle. And, who knows what would have happened after I retired if I hadn't reinvented my beliefs and my thinking.

Review those ten mantras again. Please! Do you see the collective power they provide? They are like compound interest in that each one of them by themselves is worth something, but in total, they create a multiplying effect on the brain that would be a challenge to quantify. I'm not sure that I can accurately describe how dramatically this process changed me, but thank God it did!

One other mantra I developed later went something like this: "I am a beautiful, wonderful, holy man of God. And I am creative, intelligent, and able to overcome obstacles that show up in my path to achieve my goals and dreams. There is nothing that I can't do if I desire it!"

There was a period in my life where I repeated that mantra, or some variation, 25 times in the morning and 25 times in the evening. And I did it looking in the mirror and/or holding my wife's hands and repeating it to her. It is amazing how that repetition created the changes in my brain and completely rewrote the scripts and beliefs in my mind.

As I referenced earlier, realize the important facts about your brain. It doesn't discern fact from fiction. It only knows what it perceives or what you tell it to know. So you might as well tell it the positive things that you *want* to be true and that you *want* to show up in your life.

And this takes repetition and consistency. You cannot change life-long habits and beliefs in a day or a week. In fact, the notion of changing habits in 21 days or 21 repetitions is a fallacy and couldn't be further from the truth. The 21-day myth began as a misinterpretation of Dr. Maxwell

Maltz's work on self-image. Maltz, a cosmetic surgeon, wrote the book *Psycho-Cybernetics* in 1960, but he did *not* find that 21 days of task completion forms a habit.[4]

If it's something simple like moving your wastebasket to the other side of the room, then, yes, you can change the habit of tossing paper into the basket in 21 repetitions or less. But life and your brain aren't that simple. Understand that you have built super-neural highways in your brain that have to be completely rebuilt with new pavement and new signposts, and that doesn't happen overnight, or with 21 repetitions. Please don't be discouraged by my discounting the notion of 21 repetitions. I want you to be realistic in understanding two things: (1) *You can reinvent and completely change your belief systems*, and (2) *It will take time, effort, and consistency.* And maybe in 21 repetitions—maybe not.

After considering and developing mantras that may help you launch yourself in new directions, the next suggestion is to consider looking at and reviewing the successes you've had in your life. In the coaching work that I do, I find that most of us aren't documenting our successes in a meaningful way. We just assume that what we do every day is just that, what's expected. I encourage people to start documenting their accomplishments regularly—monthly at a minimum and weekly is best—so that you can begin to build your own personal track record of successes that you can go back and revisit from time to time.

I've taken my successes and leveraged them many times over to achieve even greater accomplishments—or to try something completely new, like writing a book!

Another suggestion comes from my work as well, and that is to find a coach or accountability partner just as Marshall Goldsmith prescribed in his book that I referenced earlier. I believe we all need a "guide on the side" who can help us see what we may not be able to see for ourselves and hold up the mirror when it needs holding up.

One area that many people struggle with is losing weight. In a six-month study published in the *Journal of Consulting and Clinical Psychology*, 66 percent of dieters with a social support system were able to lose weight and keep it off, while only 24 percent of those without social support were able to maintain their success.[5]

My final suggestion is linked to a Carol Dweck quote about learning and failing. She says, "This is a time of tremendous change where you're going to have periods of confusion. You're going to turn into a novice over and over again. And we need to be comfortable not only with effort, but also with struggle and confusion."[6] As I've stated, to grow, we must become comfortable being uncomfortable! The *effort* is something that we should focus on much more than winning or losing. If you give your best effort and don't win the game, you still learn something.

If you would like to pursue another thought leader on this subject of rewiring your brain and developing new beliefs, I would highly suggest that you read Shirzad Charmin's book *Positive Intelligence: Why Only 20% of Teams and Individuals Achieve Their True Potential and How You Can Achieve Yours.* His well-researched information and methodology has swept the executive coaching world and I believe the information contained in his book can add to the information presented here. It's much too involved to go into any detail here, but briefly, he describes much like I have his horrific childhood and how he learned to cope and then as an adult recognizing what he has come to call his Saboteurs and his Sages. I firmly believe that you would benefit by making his book the next book that you read!

These first five chapters of the book are the most detailed because they are the foundation for the next two chapters in this section and the other two principles. Let's repeat once more: *You become what you think about most of the time.* And, *your beliefs determine your destiny.* If you believe those two statements—really get them and own them—then the time is *now* to put into action the process of examining what and how you want to change.

POINTS TO REMEMBER

- Our core beliefs drive our emotional reactions, which in turn produce our thoughts and behavioral responses.
- By repeatedly speaking positive affirmations to yourself in the mirror, you can start to reprogram your brain into a different reality.
- You can reinvent and completely change your belief systems. It will take time, effort, and consistency.
- Find a coach or accountability partner.
- Your beliefs determine your destiny.

ACTION ITEMS

1. Develop a daily mantra that incorporates the new belief statements or what you want to rewire in your brain.
2. Commit to reading the mantra every day until the new belief is cemented into your brain.
3. Start recording your successes
4. Find an accountability partner
5. Become comfortable being uncomfortable.

CHAPTER 6

WHAT DO YOU BELIEVE ABOUT OTHER PEOPLE?

Many people think the best way they can help others is
to criticize them, to give them the benefit of their "wisdom."
I disagree. The best way to help people is to see the best in them.

—John C. Maxwell

As we shift in this section from learning about our brains and our belief system to the application of becoming an UnCommon Leader, let's look at the term "positive expectancy." What does that mean as it relates to leadership? It means a great deal to how you show up, whom you give attention to, and what kind of attention you give them. It's the beginning of the shift to a more personalized leadership approach, and it could be a game changer for us in our New Reality.

It comes down to what you truly believe about the people whom you are privileged enough to lead. Another element of the question of what you believe about other people has to do with your beliefs and perceptions of other people, and more specifically, certain people.

We are all familiar with biases, both conscious and unconscious, but those same biases how can greatly influence how we lead others. The first psychologist to systematically study the issue of how and what you think about others or a specific person was a Harvard professor named Robert Rosenthal, who in 1964 did an experiment at an elementary school south of San Francisco. The idea was to figure out what would happen if teachers were told that certain kids in their class were destined to succeed, so Rosenthal took a normal IQ test and dressed it up as a different test. Alex Spiegel reported on the experiment in a segment for NPR in 2012:

> "It was a standardized IQ test, Flanagan's Test of General Ability," he says. "But the cover we put on it, we had printed on every test booklet, said, 'Harvard Test of Inflected Acquisition.'"
>
> Rosenthal told the teachers that this very special test from Harvard had the very special ability to predict which kids were about to be very special—that is, which kids were about to experience dramatic growth in their IQ.
>
> After the kids took the test, he then chose from every class several children totally at random. There was nothing at all to distinguish these kids from the other kids, but he told their teachers that the test predicted the kids were on the verge of an intense intellectual bloom.
>
> As he followed the children over the next two years, Rosenthal discovered that the teacher's expectations of these kids did affect the students. "If teachers had been led to expect greater gains in IQ, then increasingly, those kids gained more IQ," he says.
>
> But just how do expectations influence IQ?
>
> As Rosenthal did more research, he found that expectations affect teachers' *moment-by-moment interactions with the children they teach in a thousand almost invisible ways.*
>
> Teachers give the students that they expect to succeed more time to answer questions, more specific feedback, and more approval: They consistently touch, nod, and smile at those kids more.[1]

So it is with all of us and how we "expect" people to show up and to whom and what kind of attention we give. What do you really believe about that person? Do you have high expectations for them? Or do you believe that no matter what tools or education you give them, there is a ceiling to their performance?

In the world of leadership, Jean Francios Manzoni, the President of IMD in Lausanne, Switzerland did his Ph.D. on the same topic, the "Pygmalion Effect," that Dr. Rosenthal did with students and teachers. He and his co-author researched the Pygmalion Effect and how it relates to the way one treats and leads other people. The essence of Manzoni's book, co-written with Jean-Louis Barsoux, and titled *The Set-Up-To-Fail Syndrome,*[2] is that how we treat others is directly related to what we believe about them—whether we believe they are a low performer or a high performer. He estimates that up to 90 percent of leaders divide their teams into "in-groups" and "out-groups." What do we know about the brain and people in general? That we have a deep desire to belong. We want to be valued. If you think about yourself as a leader, and you either consciously or subconsciously label certain people in the out-group, what are you creating?

You are creating a very unsafe place to be, and you've lit up the area of their brain to be worried, concerned, and focused on the fear of failure versus the opportunities to succeed. This is on you, dear leader!

Here's a question: Has this ever happened to you, having a boss you knew didn't trust you, and you could see that they were treating you very differently than others? If it has, then you can relate to exactly what I'm saying.

While I started the book off with my story of being asked to lead the largest division of our company and how it dramatically and positively affected me, the story has another side that represents this phenomenon. Soon after we sold our company in May 2007, my CEO came to me and asked me to step down as president of the division I had been leading. Was it a performance issue? Absolutely not. Our division was doing quite well. To his credit, he was very loyal to those people who had helped him build the company and position it for a successful sale. If you know anything about mergers and acquisitions, especially between two publicly traded companies, the pressure to produce accretive earnings as quickly as possible is paramount.

And we also know there are several areas of any company that are easy targets for duplication of roles, which can mean pink slips and a quick reduction in headcount. One of those areas is accounting and finance, and the reason I was asked to step down and move into a different role was so that our CFO could have a job as he was no longer needed in that role since the acquiring company had a very qualified CFO.

To say that the move crushed me would be an understatement. A few months after the big change, I crashed and burned. I was diagnosed with total adrenal failure. I had just enough energy to wake up in the morning and stay somewhat alert, but only for about three hours. Then it was crash time again driven by the extreme drop in my hormone levels. My doctor wanted me to go out on long-term disability, but I chose to work part-time while trying to recover.

When it became apparent that I was no longer able to contribute to the company in the manner I had for the previous 13 years, I suddenly found myself in the out-group with our CEO. How I was treated from that point became very different.

One key point—my CEO never even told the Chairman and the CEO of the acquiring company that I was sick! That is unbelievable, but it's true. And it's an amplification of what Dr. Manzoni wrote. I no longer cared at the same level that I cared before. Not just because I was sick but also because of how I was being treated. We did this crazy game for about six months until we finally agreed on an exit plan for me, and I left the company about eight months after the diagnosis. The epilogue is that it took me almost two years to completely heal and get well from the adrenal failure.

Many leadership experts attempt to apply the Pareto Principle to working with and dealing with low performers. Their view is that you'll end up spending 80 percent of your time on the 20 percent of people who probably aren't going to change. This especially is applied by sales managers to their salespeople.

I understand the argument they are making. But the point I believe they are missing is that it's possible that a different approach—far from spending 80 percent of your time—would achieve different results. I'm a believer in the idea that we should review this concept first before arbitrarily deciding that some people are low performers and, therefore, we're done with them.

So if our view of people is a direct predictor of how we treat them, then what is the first step in dealing with low performers? The intervention begins with us—you and me. We must first be willing to change *our* view of the person and believe (there's that word again) the person has potential.

One executive I was coaching wanted to work on his relationship with one of his peers. He dreaded going to one-on-one meetings with this person because, "They always end up being contentious."

We worked through some discussions, but then I asked him these questions: "What's your mindset when you are getting ready for the meeting? What are your expectations? What's your body doing when you start preparing for the meeting?"

He acknowledged that he tensed up. He got jittery. And he "expected" the meeting to go badly. "Great awareness," I told him! So, he changed his mindset and his expectations as well as the questions he developed to keep the meeting on a positive track. And, he anticipated a great, productive meeting. The first meeting after he refocused his mind and his thinking about the person was an extraordinary event for him. He was amazed at how productive and positive the meeting went and how simply changing his mental state and then reframing his expectations of the meeting and of the person in the meeting created a totally different tenor and outcome. He applied the concept of assuming positive intent and it worked!

Our approach to leading and managing people is imperative. It's the age-old statement but applied to leading people: If you keep doing what you've always done, you'll keep getting what you've always gotten.

POINTS TO REMEMBER

- How you treat another person is directly related to what you believe about them—whether you believe they are a low performer or a high performer.
- As a good leader, you must be willing to change your view of a person and believe the person has potential first—then there is the potential for transformation.

CHAPTER 7

WHAT DO YOU BELIEVE ABOUT CHANGE AND THE CONNECTION TO TALENT DEVELOPMENT?

Change is only another word for growth,
another synonym for learning.

—Charles Handy

I'm often asked, "Ed, can people really change?" And, "If you believe they can change, what does it take? Is there some secret formula?"

In case you haven't noticed, most of the world has had to deal with abundant change in the recent past. The Covid pandemic has created change that we couldn't have imagined, and it's been forced upon us whether we wanted it or not. In most cases that change has been radical. Couples who both work and have school-age kids have been forced to figure out how to juggle work and home schooling. Some companies and organizations closed their doors, leaving people unemployed. The amount of change thrust upon the world is probably not measurable, but we have all lived through it at some level. Just as that phone call I received the night of March 3, 2020, radically disrupted my world, each of us has experienced a level of change we could not have imagined before Covid happened.

When I am asked that question, "Can people change?" I have a concrete, yet silly, analogy that I believe accurately portrays what is possible: I don't believe a cat can become a dog, but I believe a cat can learn dog tricks with focused, intentional effort, along with a great coach. An *America's Got Talent* episode in 2018 featured exactly that—a cat doing dog tricks![1]

To use this analogy as our basis for the idea that we can learn new tricks, let's address the concept of how we approach change. As this section has identified, the first step is to evaluate your personal beliefs about change and about the stories you've created regarding change for yourself, your family, and possibly the people you work with. And if you are a leader of other people, then the previous chapter regarding Manzoni's work on how you treat your people is a possible harbinger into your beliefs about whether people can change. It is critical that you understand your mindset because without the belief that you and other people can truly change who you and they are and what you and they do day in and day out, any effort at change will be sabotaged from the start.

I encourage you to adopt what Carol Dweck calls the "growth mindset" versus the "fixed mindset."[2] What is a growth mindset as Dweck describes it? It is having the belief that your talents can be developed through hard work, good strategies, and input from others. When we have this growth mindset, we tend to achieve more than those who have a more fixed mindset—those who believe their talents are innate gifts. If a leader, and even an entire company, can embrace a growth mindset, their employees report feeling far more empowered and committed. They also receive far greater organizational support for collaboration and innovation.

How does this mindset play out with our abilities and attitudes about change? I believe that most of us have heard the expression, and maybe you've even stated this yourself, that people resist change. To me, this statement is too broad and needs to be looked at in the context of us as individuals, or to use a refrain from the book, viewed as personal and personalized.

What I have discovered, and what you'll learn more about in the third section when I go into detail about the Birkman Method® assessment, is that people can approach change in very different ways. The assessment uses a scale of 1 to 99 for measuring intensity. One equals low intensity and 99 equals high intensity.

A person scoring a 1 on the components that measure change would be a person who would not want change and would probably resist change unless they decided it was the right thing to do, and even then, they may not act. But the 99s are ready, willing, and able to change on a dime. "Bring it on" might be their mantra. As you read this, you are probably thinking about yourself and others you know who align with those extremes or fall somewhere in between.

In the Covid world we lived in, this played out in the marketplace, and we all saw the extremes. I know people who hunkered down and took drastic measures to isolate themselves to avoid getting Covid. I also know people who continued to live life as usual and refused to accept that they couldn't do what they were doing before. These attitudes and approaches could be on the classic bell curve in that ten percent of people may fall in the very low-score category of resisting change (<10), and ten percent are in the high-score category (>90), while the rest of the world is somewhere between ten and 90. The point is that you can't label everyone with a statement that people resist change, or they resist the pain of change. Again, this is personal, and I encourage you to reflect on yourself and where you might be on that scale from 1 to 99. The importance of being able to accept change can't be overstated when it comes to personal leadership development. The phrase I've mentioned before, which is critical to change and growth, is that we must get comfortable being uncomfortable if we are to move forward, grow in our leadership abilities, and accept that we might fail at times as we transform certain aspects of our mindset, skills, and abilities.

This question of how people approach change relates very closely to our ability to develop and acquire new skills and talents as well. When we talk about change, finding hidden talents, and adding skills and abilities, the fundamental question we are asking is: What does it take to reinvent or move in new directions in life? The New Reality we've been experiencing has required many of us to evaluate where we are, what we are doing, and whether we need to make significant changes.

The first thing to explore when we look at developing new talents and skills is the question of whether talent (or leadership) is based on nature or nurture. Are we born with the ability to be a great leader, or do we have to develop those skills? I believe that leaders are made and not born, as proven by Anders Ericsson in his research and publications on talent development. He's the father of the concept of it taking 10,000 hours to develop a talent or skill.

There have been many books written by other authors using his re- search to extol the virtues of this concept. His research suggests that talent is 95 percent developed and five percent inherent. That may be a stunning fact for most people, and I've verified this by numerous speeches I've done where I ask the audience what they think about talent development—is it developed or is it innate? Even for those who know some version of this information, most people are stunned to hear that research bears out that it could be as much as 95 percent developed.

Ericcson's research shows us the fact that there are three factors to developing talent (or change): (1) practice, (2) practice with a coach, (3) deliberate practice.[3] What is deliberate practice? Practicing what you *don't* know how to do. It means getting comfortable being uncomfortable. I also believe that there are two caveats to Ericsson's research.

The first is that there are windows of opportunity for acquiring or becoming talented in certain areas. We can't unilaterally suggest that with enough belief you can do *anything* you desire to do, become *anything* that you want to become, or develop *any* talent or skill at an expert level. I un- derstand that this might sound as if I'm contradicting earlier discussions about changing your beliefs but hang with me and I'll explain.

For example, I can still shoot the "J," meaning the basketball in the hoop. When I shoot hoops, I make about 50 percent of my shots from inside the three-point line and about 40 percent outside the line. Pretty good stats. Let's say I wake up tomorrow and tell my wife, "Eva, I'm going to become an NBA basketball player. I'm going to hire a coach and work out, and by this time next year, I'll be on the roster of an NBA team." Guess what? It's not going to happen! I'm a seasoned veteran (euphemism for an "old guy!) and I'm about 5'9". Try as I might, work hard, practice, and practice with a coach, I'll never be able to make an NBA roster. Heck, I might not even be able to make a YMCA team of 20- and 30-year-olds, much less a team of the most talented people on the planet in that sport. So we do have limitations that can block our achievement of certain goals. No matter how much we desire or believe those things, they just aren't going to happen.

The second caveat is that I do believe that there are certain aspects of ourselves that are naturally inherited through our genes. We know that we might receive traits from our genes, like hair color, eye color, and our height. Another possible trait we receive is hand-eye coordination. The example I use is Tiger Woods. Tiger's father had a goal in mind from day one—that Tiger was going to be a professional golfer. What if his father had decided he was going to help Tiger become a professional tennis player, and instead of a golf club he gave him a tennis racket when he was six months old? I believe that Tiger would have been competing with Pete Sampras and Roger Federer for major tennis titles. Why? Because I truly believe that one of the factors Tiger was born with is his hand-eye coordination. I don't have proof of that, but I do have an experience that is a strong indicator this could be an inherited trait.

I saw this play out years ago in our neighborhood. I have a unique talent that I developed as a child with lots of practice, and, again I believe that I was born with great hand-eye coordination that helped me excel quickly as evidenced by my abilities to do things with balls, toys, and games that other kids my age struggled with. Because of that I became a bit of an expert with Duncan spin tops. If you know what those are, you're probably like me, a seasoned veteran! I competed in tournaments around the city of Charleston and accumulated patches from wins and placing in tournaments. Even today, I can pick up a Duncan spin top and still do the tricks I did as a seven-to-ten-year-old boy.

It started when we were having a block party in our neighborhood, and I brought out my tops and started doing tricks for the kids. Quite a few of them wanted to learn how to do the basic first skill of tossing the top so it lands on the ground and keeps spinning. I got the kids in a line and started teaching each of them. The first boy learned easily and quickly; he accomplished the feat on the second try. But two kids, no matter what I said or had them do, just couldn't make the top spin on the ground. Their lack of hand-eye coordination was obvious, especially in contrast to the first child. Could they have learned? Probably. But this is the point: Several of them showed very easy and natural hand-eye coordination that accelerated their learning and skill level. Others didn't have the same talent to catch up with them.

If you've read Malcolm Gladwell's book *Outliers*, then you may realize that he leveraged much of Ericcson's work on talent development but went further in describing these windows of opportunity and that some people may have had more natural attributes, as well as timely opportunities, that enabled them to excel.[4]

The bottom line is that *most* of the goals and objectives we want to set for ourselves are within our reach if we apply the right mindset and find the right resources to help us achieve those goals and objectives. Just as I referenced earlier in this section and in this chapter, for the most part, *if you believe you can or if you believe that you can't, you're right.*

The secret ingredients are motivation and willingness to be a novice and fail before we acquire the new talent, habit, or skill. We each have the ability to acquire new knowledge, skills, and talents if we desire them strongly enough, find the right assistance, and stick to it.

We *do* have unlimited potential and can access many more talents, skills, and competencies—if we have the willingness to fail before we succeed. As leaders, we must embrace this mindset about ourselves and the people we lead. And we must bring this mindset to the topic of change and recognize that change is a necessary part of our existence and important to our growth and development. You can embrace change. You can become a change agent if you desire to grow and become an UnCommon Leader.

Failing is only failure if we don't learn from it, pick ourselves up, and try again—and keep doing that until we have achieved our goals.

POINTS TO REMEMBER

- Without the belief that you and other people can truly change, any effort at change could be sabotaged from the start.
- Adopt the "growth mindset" and rid yourself of the "fixed mindset."
- We must get comfortable being uncomfortable if we are to move forward, grow in our leadership abilities, and accept that we might fail at times as we transform certain aspects of our mindset, skills, and abilities.
- If you believe you can or you believe that you can't, you're right!

LEADERSHIP STARTS WITH YOUR BELIEFS

The Covid pandemic challenged many of us to dig deep, make lemons from lemonade as best as we could, and reset our mind's eye on what is important. Our beliefs about ourselves, our families, and our workplaces have been challenged. If you take nothing else from this section, please understand two things: 1) Your beliefs are incredibly important and can determine your destiny, and 2) you can rewrite your beliefs to empower you to greater heights, whatever that may look like for you.

Let's finish up this section with a comment about your belief system, especially as it relates to the story about my brother and his liver cancer diagnosis. If all that you and I had to do was be positive and believe that we would be healed from any disease, there would be no sickness in the world. Just being positive isn't the answer. In fact, Tony Robbins was quoted in an interview that being positive is BS! If ever there were someone that many believe could have the label of "Mr. Positive" it's Robbins. His rationale is this: If you have weeds in your garden, you can't stand there and with positive statements get rid of the weeds. You must *do* something in order to get them out of the garden. This is the essence of the message I've tried to communicate in this section: You are in control of what you believe, but it takes work and effort to rewrite the scripts and set the navigation system for another destination.

I read an article about a woman who had been diagnosed many years earlier with metastasized breast cancer. It seemed that all her well-meaning friends had plenty of advice for her, mostly unsolicited, and the resounding theme was to "be positive." During her terrible battle, she found it hard to be positive. Finally, a trusted source helped her see that it wasn't about being positive and chanting "I'm positive, I'm positive," 25 times a day. It was about accepting her situation and doing the best she could do with the treatments she received. The interesting thing was that once she let go of trying to be positive, she found hope and became more positive.

And that is what we all need—*hope!* Each of us should have some idea of what that looks like for ourselves, our families, our co-workers, and our friends. One of my favorite Scripture verses is in the book of Proverbs. "*Where there is no vision, the people perish*" (Proverbs 29:18, KJV). Consider that King Solomon was considered to be the wisest person on the planet during his time. And this quote leads us to the second section.

PRINCIPLE 2

LEADERSHIP REQUIRES 20/20 VISION

PRINCIPLE
1
**LEADERSHIP STARTS
WITH YOUR BELIEFS**

PRINCIPLE
2
**LEADERSHIP REQUIRES
20/20 VISION**

PRINCIPLE
3
**LEADERSHIP IS IN THE
EYE OF THE BEHOLDER**

CHAPTER 8

DO YOU KNOW WHERE YOU'RE GOING?

*It's been said that the gate of history turns
on small hinges, and so do people's lives.
The choices we make determine our destiny.*

—Thomas S. Monson

The quote by Monson is powerful and indicates that we must get intentional about where we are going and what we want our lives to mean. And we find one of the most poignant lessons regarding the need for vision in the 1951 Disney movie, *Alice In Wonderland,*[1] based on Lewis Carroll's *Alice's Adventures in Wonderland.* As Alice is strolling through the garden, she encounters a fork in the road. Peering down from high up in the tree is the Cheshire cat, and she sees an opportunity for guidance from him. Here's the exchange:

"Would you tell me, please, which way I ought to go from here?"

"That depends a good deal on where you want to get to," said the cat.

"I don't much care where," said Alice.

"Then it doesn't matter which way you go," said the cat.

Reread the cat's last statement again and take in the essence and meaning. If you don't care where you're going, then it doesn't matter what road or direction you take. If you're reading this book, you probably care about where you're going. My goal is to give you guidance on how to determine where you're going and how to get there. Or maybe at some point in your life you've developed a clear vision for where you want to go and what you want to accomplish but now realize that the events created by the Covid crisis have caused you, like so many of us, to question and desire to gain even greater clarity. I do believe that this section will provide a solid foundation for you as you explore your values, vision, and mission.

I have a go-to *Harvard Business Review* article that I use in my coaching work. It's by John Kotter and the title is "Leading Change."[2] I am also a big fan of Posner and Kouze's work in their multi-edition book *The Leadership Challenge*.[3] Why do I mention them together? Because both present vision as a primary goal and initiative in their systems and models. One has it for leading change, and the other has it for great leadership. I am following their lead in that I believe the first section you've just finished reading is a crucial foundation that must be explored and solidified before moving to the concept of finding a mission and vision for yourself as a person and as a leader. I am a huge mission and vision person because I've seen the power and the results of doing the work to determine the vision for yourself and your organization or business unit.

In the New Reality more people than ever are evaluating what they are doing and what they believe in—and at a deeper level than they previously did. They are also questioning if they are being true to their values and if the vision they have for their lives (assuming they have taken the time to determine that vision) is still aligned with who they are and the difference they want to make in their own lives and the lives of others. Even if they haven't determined their own personal mission and vision, there is often a dissonance wrestling inside of them and a voice telling them something is off kilter. They are investigating that voice to determine how to solve the riddle in their life—how to find meaning and purpose.

In the Introduction's graph of the Gartner study, one key statistic is that 62 percent of respondents said that they "long for a bigger change in my life." From an article explaining Gartner's research:

This longing for a bigger change is one of the key reasons we are experiencing the global disruption of the workplace and employees continue to resign from their jobs in record numbers each month. And this bigger change, in my opinion, is just what I referenced—whether people realize it or not they are searching for meaning and purpose.[4]

Another quote from the article illuminates what is happening:

"This is a liminal period of transition, one in which people are equalized by some external force but the outcome has yet to be determined. We're all questioning our before and after states. We're asking ourselves; *Can I go back to doing what I did before in the same way? With family, travel, work, life? Should I? My well-being relies on my ability to innovate, imagine a new future, and take steps toward it, but what should that future look like?*"

The shifts are obvious, but in no way are they complete. The New Reality has opened the door for many of us to examine if we are aligned with thevalues, vision and mission of our organizations. As we've seen historic numbers of people leave their jobs and even change careers, the Gartner study provides compelling data to reveal the mindsets of people.

One of the industries hit the hardest by the Great Resignation is the restaurant and hospitality industry. Here's a chart for the US Bureau of Labor Statistics from September 2021.[5]

INDUSTRIES WITH HIGHEST PERCENTAGES OF WORKERS QUITTING

The number of quits rose to a record high of 4.4 million in September 2021.

Industry	Percentage
Leisure and hospitality	6.4%
Trade, transportation, and utilities	3.6%
Professional and business services	3.3%
Other services	3.1%
Education and health services	2.8%
Manufacturing	2.7%
Construction	2.5%
Mining and logging	1.5%
Information	1.5%
Financial activities	1.5%
Government	1%

A vivid example from the city of St. Louis is an Italian restaurant on The Hill, the famous Italian section of the city. This restaurant closed its doors after more than 40 years of being in business because of the lack of staffing. Is that a vision issue? Yes, I believe it is as the proprietors just couldn't staff the restaurant at the level that was needed to provide sufficient customer service and food quality. Many people who have worked in restaurants are looking to find their true calling and not settle for something that doesn't align with their personal values and vision. Yes, it could be a pay issue as well, but many restaurants have drastically increased the rate of pay for staff, so that isn't the single reason this industry has been affected at the level it has. But my belief is that this time period could be called the Great Awakening in that it amplifies the lesson from the *Alice in Wonderland* exchange—many of us have decided to figure out where we are going and are therefore determining which road we should travel. From my perspective, this is the bigger issue that all industries and companies are facing, which has created the massive resignations on a continual basis.

To amplify how important vision is for each of us individually and as organizations, I was giving a talk to a Society for Human Resource Management chapter, and I presented a slide of 13 years of Gallup data on employee engagement. I then asked, "Take a look at the data. Does anyone have an observation?"

Almost immediately a hand went up and the person shouted, "Nothing's changed."

I said, "Exactly." I then said, "I'm curious about something. I have a lot of respect for Gallup, and I believe they do great work. But I wonder if we're asking the right questions? If they're still saying that only 30 percent of the people in companies in America are engaged, are we even measuring the right data?"

Think about the amount of money organizations spend on leadership development and employee engagement. Leadership training is an estimated $366 billion global industry. But data provided by McKinsey offers a startling insight into the leadership industry: Most of these leadership programs fail to create the desired results.[6] This is hard to understand. Companies are investing heavily in an attempt to drive employee engagement, yet the results aren't there. Why? Maybe it isn't necessarily a training issue. Maybe it's a vision issue. Or we're not measuring the right data.

Not long after that talk to the SHRM group, I found a study from IBM that shed a completely different light and perspective on the issue of employee engagement, and they provided data to back up what they found to be the true driver of employee engagement.

Here's the truth about IBM's study. It was published to dispel some of Gallup's data and some of their theories and statements about engagement. In fact, the name of the study is "Three Myths of Employee Engagement and Leadership."[7]

For example, one of Gallup's favorite statements is that people don't quit companies, they quit bosses. While the IBM study tackles that statement head on and provides data to back up why they think it's not true, I believe that this may not be an "either/or" but a "yes, and." Gallup's data is relevant, and they have research to back their view just as IBM has research to back theirs. And in my opinion one of the key factors of the Great Resignation is lousy bosses. So, I'm not ready to throw Gallup's data out of the window because of IBM's study.

Robert Sutton, a Stanford Engineering School professor, wrote a 2007 book titled *The No Asshole Rule: Building a Civilized Workplace and Surviving One That Isn't.*[8] In the book, Sutton cites a Swedish study that was also referenced in a *Forbes* article entitled "Why Your Bad Boss Could Be Killing You," by Caroline Castrillon, who wrote:

> A survey of 3,122 employees in Sweden found that those who work for toxic bosses were 60% more likely to suffer a stroke, heart attack or other life-threatening cardiac condition. Other studies show that people with bad bosses are more susceptible to chronic depression, stress, and anxiety, all of which increase the risk of a lowered immune system. Some research even indicates that it takes people 22 months to restore their stress levels to a healthy range after working for a bad manager.[9, 10]

I believe these references clearly present to us that Gallup's data is, in fact, valuable and can be validated and could be one of the key factors in the Great Resignation. But what we are here to discover in this section is that personal and organizational vision and mission are a critical success factor and should be an exercise that each of us attends to for ourselves and the people whom we lead.

What I am hearing in the learning and development arenas from other organizations and coaches is that companies are awake at a level that we've never seen before regarding finally investing in their employees, and especially those who lead others. I'm reminded of the meme below that has made the rounds on LinkedIn and other sites for many years.

CFO TO CEO: "WHAT HAPPENS IF WE INVEST IN DEVELOPING OUR PEOPLE AND THEN THEY LEAVE US?"

CEO TO CFO: "WHAT HAPPENS IF WE DON'T, AND THEY STAY?"

We have arrived at a point in time where the issue of developing our employees can no longer take a back seat to earnings, capital expenditures, or acquisitions. This seminal moment we're in is changing the game of leadership and talent development—and it's about time!

Back to the IBM study. Their research over a five year period concluded that *the number one driver of employee engagement is the leadership's vision for the future*, or as they called it, *"leadership future vision."* If leaders can articulate a vision for where the company, business unit, or team is heading, then people can easily determine if that vision aligns with their personal values and where they want to go. If so, they will stay, even with a bad boss. If not, they will leave whether they have a bad or good boss.

A vision can provide hope for the future—a better future or a future employees can see benefiting them. IBM's study states that leaders having and articulating that vision could override an employee's desire to leave the company because of a bad boss. Since the IBM study was completed many years prior to Covid, I'm not sure that statement is 100 percent true now, and I've given you some evidence to suggest that it isn't. But I do believe it could be a huge factor in driving retention in organizations, and that is why we'll explore it deeper in this section.

The IBM study now confirms what so many people are discovering and questioning—*Do my values and vision for myself* (assuming they know what they are) *align with the values and vision of my boss, the team, my department, or the company?*

Leadership starts with you and me, and it requires us to have a vision and mission for ourselves. Do you have a mission and vision for your group, your department, your company? If you don't, why would anyone follow you? If leadership's future vision is one of the main factors driving employee engagement, then you must address this and determine why you are here, where you are going, and how you're going to get there. Then people can say, "I love where you're going as a leader, I want to be part of that." Or if that vision doesn't align with what is important to them, they can wisely remove themselves.

The concept of establishing and having a vision encompasses your values and your mission as well. You can't very well have a vision for yourself if you don't know what your values are and what mission you're on. Let's dive in next to discovering and identifying your values.

POINTS TO REMEMBER

- The number one driver of employee engagement is the leadership's vision for the future.
- A vision can provide hope for the future—a better future or a future that employees can see benefiting them.
- Do you have a vision for yourself? Can you articulate it succinctly?
- Do you have a vision for your group, your department, your company? If so, is everyone on board with the vision and do they believe in it?

CHAPTER 9

START WITH YOUR VALUES

When your values are clear to you,
making decisions becomes easier.

—Roy Disney

Have you ever thought through and put down on paper what your values are? Even if you have, can you define what those values mean? I've found that most people can state what they are when asked, but they haven't cemented them by doing the additional work of writing them down and then defining what they look like in meaningful words. We should take the time and use this method to crystalize what our values are. Another word for our values could be "non-negotiables," or as Ken Blanchard calls them, "valuables." One of the most important aspects of this process is that if we have established our values and defined exactly what they mean, we can then determine what to say yes or no to.

Early in my career I accepted a new role as a major account manager with a company. The general manager I reported to was going over some of the existing accounts I would be responsible for, and when he got to a very large, important company, he mentioned that the main contact at this company whom I would work with and had to keep satisfied liked to go to strip joints after an evening dinner. I verified just how important this account was for the company. I then told the GM that if that was the case, he himself needed to keep the account because I wasn't going to take anyone to a strip joint. He argued profusely with me and kept making the case in very shallow, general terms as to why I needed to sacrifice my values. It was an interesting situation, but if I hadn't taken the time to fully understand what my values were, I might have given in to the pressure since it was a new company with a new boss. For me it was an easy choice because that was a non-negotiable for me. But how many people might have given in if they weren't crystal clear on their values and what was non-negotiable?

How can we discover what our values are? I've provided a list of potential values on the next page for you, and here's the process I recommend for you to follow: First read over the entire list and see what resonates for you. Also think about other values I might not have listed that are important to you and write those in on the blank lines.

Second, after you've read and thought through the entire list, circle 10 to 12 of the values that are most important to you. Think about what your life would look like and how you would respond if each value were not part of who you are. For most people, this first pass can be a challenge because when you read the entire list, 20 to 25 of them may resonate with you. But just like core beliefs, we're looking for your core values, those values that you would be willing to fight for—just as in my story.

The third step is to narrow the list down to your top five values. Why five? There's no magic in that number, but I believe that every person holds somewhere between three to seven deep values that act as the foundation for the other values. Again, I use the term "non-negotiables" for those five values that make up the essence and core of your being.

And for you to do the fun exercise I'm about to describe, you need to settle on five as the final number of values.

VALUES CHECKLIST

Authenticity	Accountability	Achievement	Adaptability
Adventure	Altruism	Ambition	Alignment
Accomplishment	Participation	Acknowledgement	Learning
Balance	Beauty	Being the best	Belonging
Courage	Compassion	Certainty	Clarity
Commitment	Collaboration	Creativity	Community
Career	Competence	Confidence	Connection
Contribution	Cooperation	Curiosity	Contentment
Directness	Dignity	Diversity	Efficiency
Empathy	Excellence	Environment	Equality
Empowerment	Friendship	Family	Faith
Financial stability	Fun	Future generations	Freedom
Fairness	Generosity	Giving back	Gratitude
Growth	Harmony	Humor	Health
Honesty	Hope	Humility	Happiness
Inclusion	Intuition	Integrity	Independence
Justice	Job security	Joy	Knowledge
Kindness	Lack of pretense	Leadership	Loyalty
Money	Making a difference	Meaning	Nature

Nurturing	Orderliness	Optimism	Performance
Productivity	Privacy	Patience	Patriotism
Perseverance	Power	Pride	Recognition
Resolve	Respect	Responsibility	Risk-taking
Rules	Security	Safety	Self-discipline
Success	Spirituality	Stewardship	Service to others
Success	Teamwork	Thrift	Trust
Tradition	To be of value	Travel	Resilience
Truth	Understanding	Vulnerability	Wisdom
Wellbeing	Vision	Wealth	Passion
Truth	Beliefs	Peace	Love

Other Values Not Listed: _____

_____

MY TOP 5 VALUES

1. _____
2. _____
3. _____
4. _____
5. _____

The final step to determine your number-one value requires that you get a stack of five sticky notes and write one value on each one. When you're done, you should have five sticky notes with one value on each note. We are about to play a game, and I will remind you repeatedly that this is just a game and it's not reality.

Now imagine that you will receive gifts. But each time you receive a gift, you must tear up one of these five values on the sticky note and throw it in the wastebasket. And you may not take it back; it's gone…forever!

The first gift you receive is a one-month, all-expenses-paid vacation to the location of your dreams where you can bring up to nine more family and friends with you. Everything you've wanted to do on a vacation is now at your disposal, but you must give up one of your values. Wad it up and toss it away. Remember it's just a game. You are now left with four values.

Now for your second gift. You receive the home of your dreams in the location of your dreams, complete with a staff of people to meet and serve your every need for the rest of your life. But you must give up another value. Review the four that are left. Crumple up and toss another one away. You are down to three values. It's just a game, remember!

As an interlude, here's a brief story you may relate to. I was doing this exercise with a group of about 30 managers for a major retailer. When we got to the third gift, a lady in the group folded her arms and stated, "I'm not playing this game anymore. These are my values, and I'm not giving them up no matter what." I reminded her it was just a game so we could see what was her most important value, but I was unable to persuade her to continue playing the game. She was resolute, and I had successfully hit a nerve by asking her to give up her values. That's how powerful your values can be—you can't let go of them even if it's just a game!

Ready for your third gift? You are now to receive the career or job of your choice with the remuneration you want. No exceptions. You pick the career, you pick the role, and you pick the income no matter how incredibly large it is. But when you do, throw away one more of your values. Remember this is just a game, and you still have your final two values.

Your two most important values remain—the final two that you believe you live your life for and would fight to preserve. This is the hardest part of the game we're playing, but now you are about to receive the winning numbers to a $600 million lottery jackpot. Never again will you have to worry about money. You can do whatever you want to do. But you must give up one of those values. Which one will you crumple up and throw away? It's a hard choice even though it's not real.

Are you at the same point that the lady in the story was—done—not going to play the game anymore? If so, I get it. And that is my hope.

My #1 Value: _____

I've used this game in numerous workshops around the globe, and it's fascinating to see the different reactions. Some people have no problem throwing away their values. I can remember the reverse of the previous story when one executive quickly figured out where the game was going and couldn't wait to get to that final value to find out what he was going to get. He just tossed those wadded up sticky notes as fast as he could. But others do dig in and quit playing the game. Now that you have your top five values, it's time to investigate them by describing what they mean to you.

POINTS TO REMEMBER

- Values assist us in what to say yes or no to. They are your non-negotiables.
- Identify your top five values and then identify your number-one value.

CHAPTER 10

DEFINING YOUR VALUES

It's one thing to know what your values are.
It's quite another to define them in a manner
that allows for no ambiguity
in what you say yes to and how you live your life.

—Ed Chaffin

Here's a true story that demonstrates how we can have the same values as another person, but they mean something entirely different to each of us. I was working with a group of commercial realtors, and we had completed the exercise described in the previous chapter. I asked a man I'll call Richard what his number-one value was, and he proudly stated, "Family!"

Upon hearing this, I saw from my peripheral vision another person flinch with some negative body language. I turned to this other person I'll call Ray and asked what his number-one value was. He proudly stated, "Family!" I then told him I had seen his reaction when Richard stated that family was his most important value, and I asked him what was going on. His response was classic. And it reminds us that we can have the exact same value, but what it means to us can be *very* different, and more importantly, we judge others based on *our* definition of that value.

He explained that he viewed Richard as a workaholic, and he couldn't believe that family was that important to him. I then asked Richard how he would define, and how he lived out his value of, family. He responded that he had grown up very poor and had determined that he was going to make something of himself and be highly successful. He said, "I don't want my family to go through what I went through. I never had anything other kids had growing up, so I work my rear end off to provide for my family what I never had."

I looked at Ray and asked him how he defined and lived out his value of family. He proudly stated that most nights he was home for dinner with his family, he coached his kid's soccer and baseball teams, they went to church together, and being together as a family was far more important to him than working his rear end off to give them more money.

There you have it, two people with the same value, yet living it out in completely different ways. If you completed the previous exercise and have your top five values now, it's time to drill down and describe exactly how those values are lived out and what they mean so there is no ambiguity when the time arises to live out that value—or shift it—due to circumstances or life changes.

Here are a few values and their definitions from people that I've worked with:

- Family—I will always remember those who have made a difference in my life, and I strive to make a difference in theirs.
- Integrity—I continuously honor commitments I make to myself and to others.
- Balance—I develop the habit of happiness by investing the right amount of time into the most important areas of my life.
- Learning—I'm constantly open to new experiences and knowledge.

From this list above you should get the idea of how to do this and just how important it is to define your values. For example, some might want to be even more definitive. For example, I might add to my definition of learning, "...and take at least one new course per year to enhance my coaching knowledge and add more value to my clients."

If we are involved in a company and have the opportunity to influence and/or define values, it's imperative to define exactly what they mean as well. In a previous role I had, we sponsored an executive exchange for chief human resources officers, and I was leading a roundtable discussion when the topic of values came up. One human resources officer told the story of a failed acquisition. When the company's executives had looked at another company to possibly acquire it, one item indicating this would be a success was that the other company's website listed the same values as their own. But after acquiring the company, they realized that the *definitions* of those values were vastly different—so different that they were unable to effectively merge the two cultures. The result was a huge culture clash that spawned resignations and workforce reductions. They lived through a total nightmare simply because they couldn't integrate their mutual value definitions. In fact, we know from research that 40 to 80 percent of acquisitions fail to achieve accretive results due to the failure to integrate cultures. The disconnect between values could be a major contributing factor to that data.

With the permission of one of my clients here are their company's values and definitions:

1. **Inspiring Vision:** We believe that clear vision inspires others to accomplish audacious goals.
2. **Innovating Ways:** We believe that all things are possible and constantly innovate to find new ways to serve.
3. **Others First:** We believe that business should be more about the people we serve than about us.
4. **Integrity:** We believe that living above reproach is important in all aspects of life.
5. **Empowered Team:** We believe that empowering our team to take ownership, take risks, and solve problems leads to a better service.

In wrapping up the two chapters on values, here's information on how important this exercise can be and the benefits that can be derived. From an article in *Psychology Today* by Meg Selig,

1. Values can help you reduce stress.
2. Connecting with your values boosts decision-making and problem-solving skills.
3. Your values can inspire better health habits.
4. Values can rev up your willpower so that you can persist at different tasks.
5. Values can help you act more assertively.
6. Values can help you communicate with more compassion.
7. Remembering your values helps you make wiser career and work choices.
8. Knowing and acting on your values bolsters your confidence.
9. Knowing and sharing your values enhances relationship intimacy.[1]

If you've read the past two chapters and didn't act on the exercise of identifying and defining your values, my hope in providing the nine powerful statements above is that you see more clearly just how important and powerful this exercise can be. Do I have your attention now? I hope so!

POINTS TO REMEMBER

- Clearly define your top five values.
- Describe how you live out each of these top five values.

CHAPTER 11

CREATING THE VISION

"Don't underestimate the power of vision and direction. These are irresistible forces, able to transform what might appear to be unconquerable obstacles into traversable pathways and expanding opportunities. Strengthen the individual. Start with yourself. Take care with yourself. Define who you are. Refine your personality. Choose your destination and articulate your being. As the great nineteenth-century German philosopher Friedrich Nietzsche so brilliantly noted, 'He whose life has a why can bear almost any how.'"

—Jordan Peterson

When we know our values as a person and a leader, then it's time to move on to developing and creating the vision for ourselves or our department or company. I am a firm believer that the next step is the "Why" step and should precede the development of a mission statement. My encouragement, as you look at leadership's future vision, if you've never done any vision work on yourself, is that it can be a phenomenal, yet challenging, exercise. I've referenced several books so far that have had a huge impact on me as I reinvented my life. One of those was Stephen Covey's *The 7 Habits of Highly Successful People.*[1] And a key influence was the second chapter, "Begin With the End in Mind." Covey used the example of building a home and how you would never think about going out to your property and just starting to dig the foundation without under-standing what the final product would look like. You hire an architect and have them develop the blueprint with detailed drawings of the finished home, with several different views from which to determine if it is in fact the home of your dreams. They would outline exactly how the foundation would be, and everything else would be built on that foundation.

A true, and ultimately somewhat tragic, anecdote is that one of my dad's friends, after seeing the foundation for his new home which was completed according to the architect's specifications, didn't think it was big enough. So he had them redo the foundation to make it bigger. The result? Huge issues as the new size created a ripple effect of problems, such as carpets not coming in a large enough width to accommodate the bigger rooms, which resulted in seams in the carpet where seams shouldn't be—and they were painfully obvious in some rooms. And there were other systemic issues such as where doors were to be located, and many other issues that the soon-to-be-owner of the home discovered. This is what can happen when we don't have a firm, clear vision of what we want the re-sult to be.

One key difference with the guidance that Covey provides is that he uses the term *mission statement* the way that I use the term *vision statement*. My perspective on this has been driven by my own personal experiences of performing his recommended exercise and developing a "mission" state-ment. But as I moved through life and work, I began to realize that his version of mission was my version of vision.

The exercise that Covey provides in his book leads the reader to im-agine in rich detail getting up from your chair in your home, getting into your car, and driving to a location. Next he asks you to imagine parking your car, walking into a building and seeing a huge crowd of people, and then going to the front row of the venue and taking a seat. It is at that point in your visualization that you realize you are attending your own funeral.

As the funeral service begins, a moderator announces that four people from four different areas of your life are going to speak about you and your life, what you stood for, how you lived your life, and what you meant to them. The four areas are: (1) family, (2) close friends, (3) co-workers, and (4) community involvement. My recommendation is to get Covey's book if you haven't already. Read it and follow through on the exercises he prescribes.

I have taken several groups through this exercise. I have participants visualize each of those persons from their life and then guide them to listen to the words spoken about them. After the first person from their family has spoken, I bring the group out of the visualization and ask them to start writing as fast as they can what they heard that person say. I have them write with no thought to sentence structure, grammar, or punctuation as they write from the heart about what they saw and heard in their visualization. Then I take them back to the scene to visualize the next person, and repeat the exercise until all four people have spoken and each participant has written as much as they can. It's not an event. It is a process that I believe must be repeated as many times as necessary to fully grasp your *Why*. I do recommend that there be some gap time in between the exercises so that you can digest and process what each occurrence has produced. I don't have any magic number of times to advise you to do the exercise, but I believe that you will know when you have exhausted the process and have the necessary information to form your vision statement.

In 1992 I spent more than a year doing this same exercise over and over until clarity emerged about who I was, who I wanted to be, and what my vision was for my life. Or said another way, what my legacy would be. It turned out to be what you read earlier—changing the world one life at a time by making a difference in the lives of those I'm blessed to serve. Over time, I gained even more clarity about what that looked like, and it allowed me to make the right decisions or to realize that I was off track and reorient myself and my leadership back toward that vision.

A true story will show how valuable this exercise is. After I had developed my personal vision, I was motivated to change careers and pursue what I believed God had put me on the planet to do—leadership consulting, speaking, and coaching. In 1993 I walked away from a very good job and launched my own company. I was convinced I would be the next Tony Robbins. But I was sadly mistaken. I had not evaluated two key, critical issues before jumping into the ocean. One was how long it would take to start generating enough revenue to support my family. The second lesson was that if you're going to be an entrepreneur, you had better make sure your spouse/partner is aligned and understands the risks. The bottom line is I failed miserably, and about six months into the new venture I had to abandon the effort and go back to work for a company. Was I defeated? Yes. Did I quit and forget the vision that I had? Not in your life! A fire inside me had been lit, and it wasn't extinguished by that failure. I was disappointed, but I now had a dream that drove my vision, and I wasn't about to give it up.

What my experience taught me could be likened to what I would call reorienting or "tacking" as in the analogy of sailing. If you've sailed, or been on a sailboat, you know that sailing directly into the wind can't be done head-on because the wind will blow you backward. To move forward, you must tack back and forth at angles to the wind.

And you must have a destination in mind. I had hit a headwind, but I had the destination in mind. So I tacked for a time to develop more experience, skills, knowledge, and staying power for the next time I would jump into the ocean of leadership consulting and executive coaching.

Just like *Alice in Wonderland*, if you're on a sailboat with no destination in mind, then you're merely sailing aimlessly across the water. Nothing wrong with that if you're taking a day off. But if it's your life, don't you want to know where you're going and what that destination might look like?

POINTS TO REMEMBER

- Create, or re-imagine, your life and the vision for your life with the end in mind.
- Spend time to deeply think through these questions:

   Who are you?
   Who do you want to be?
   What will be your legacy?
   Where did you make a difference?
   Who were the people in your life?
   How did you make a difference?
   What was important to you?
   What did you say yes to?
   What did you say no to?

CHAPTER 12

COMMUNICATING YOUR VISION

Action without vision is only passing time,
vision without action is merely day-dreaming,
but vision with action can change the world!

—Nelson Mandela

You can't deliver value unless you ground yourself in values. Chew on that for a moment. This is one of the tenets of Bill George's *Discover Your True North,*[1] written to help you become an authentic leader. He views authenticity as essential to being a leader who makes a difference in the lives of others and makes the world a better place. We've already discussed the importance of establishing your core values and how to identify them and then define exactly what they mean to you. I highly recommend his book because he also goes to great lengths about discovering your true north, which is the same topic we detailed in the previous chapter—the vision for who you are or want to be.

I've looked for powerful examples of leaders who have identified a vision and are able to articulate it with an inspiring call to action. These stories establish a true north and inspire others to rally around that vision, execute it, and accomplish it. This next story is one of the best I can find.

Many of us seasoned veterans remember the space war from the 1950s and '60s. Russia fired the first shot with the launch of the Sputnik spacecraft, which completely caught the US off guard. Russia had to be countered, and we had to have a visionary leader to respond to their shot across our bow. Enter John F. Kennedy. The year was 1962, and in a speech at Rice University, he delivered his vision for the US as it related to the Space Race. Here is an extended excerpt of his speech to give you the full flavor of what setting a vision and articulating that vision sounds like (note the sailing analogy):

Yet the vows of this nation can only be fulfilled if we in this nation are first, and, therefore, we intend to be first. In short, our leadership in science and industry, our hopes for peace and security, our obligations to ourselves as well as others, all require us to make this effort, to solve these mysteries, to solve them for the good of all men, and to become the world's leading space-faring nation.

We set sail on this new sea because there is new knowledge to be gained, and new rights to be won, and they must be won and used for the progress of all people. For space science, like nuclear science and all technology, has no conscience of its own. Whether it will become a force for good or ill depends on man, and only if the United States occupies a position of pre-eminence can we help decide whether this new ocean will be a sea of peace or a new terrifying theater of war.

I do not say that we should or will go unprotected against the hostile misuse of space any more than we go unprotected against the hostile use of land or sea, but I do say that space can be explored and mastered without feeding the fires of war, without repeating the mistakes that man has made in extending his writ around this globe of ours.

There is no strife, no prejudice, no national conflict in outer space as yet. Its hazards are hostile to us all. Its conquest deserves the best of all mankind, and its opportunity for peaceful cooperation may never come again. But why, some say, the moon? Why choose this as our goal? And they may well ask why climb the highest mountain? Why, 35 years ago, fly the Atlantic? Why does Rice play Texas?

We choose to go to the moon. We choose to go to the moon (interrupted by applause) we choose to go to the moon in this decade and do the other things, not because they are easy, but because they are hard, because that goal will serve to organize and measure the best of our energies and skills, because that challenge is one that we are willing to accept, one we are unwilling to postpone, and one which we intend to win, and the others too.

It is for these reasons that I regard the decision last year to shift our efforts in space from low to high gear as among the most important decisions that will be made during my incumbency in the office of the Presidency.[2]

So, it happened that seven years later, in 1969, the US landed a crew on the moon, and Neil Armstrong became the first man on the moon, followed 19 minutes later by Buzz Aldrin. This is a prime example of a leadership future vision that drove a nation to accomplish something that many believed impossible. And it was in part inspired by John F. Kennedy's rousing speech that day.

Earlier I referenced Barry Posner and Jim Kouzes' *The Leadership Challenge*. Posner and Kouzes have been researching leadership for more than 30 years and have now completed six editions of their book. They developed The Five Practices of Exemplary Leadership Model. As I referenced earlier in this section, the number two practice is Inspire a Shared Vision. This is from their website and how they describe it:

"Leaders passionately believe they can make a difference. They envision the future and create an ideal and unique image of what the organization can become. Through their magnetism and persuasion, leaders enlist others in their dreams. They breathe life into their visions and get people to see exciting possibilities for the future."[3]

The Leadership Challenge framework for leadership amplifies that we must have a true north—a vision for ourselves, our company, or our team. If we can provide that vision, we must be able to communicate the vision in a compelling manner as in the example provided above by John F. Kennedy. In the coaching and consulting work that I've done I still find so many leaders that do not understand the power, and the purpose, of communicating your vision on a continual basis. One of my mantras when coaching executives is that you can't communicate enough. If you think you're communicating too much, keep communicating! If you don't, people will make up the stories they want to make up, and what they will make up is usually far worse than anything that you would ever tell them!

A prime example of this was an executive coaching assignment several years ago for the president of a division of a large, multi-national corporation. His division had the lowest employee engagement scores of the entire company, and I was brought in to help the executive understand what it would look like to elevate his leadership and better inspire the employees in his group.

I asked him about his communications—how often, how much, what type, etc., etc. He answered initially that every year he did a town hall meeting for all employees, and in that meeting he outlined the key initiatives, goals, and objectives for the upcoming year. I then asked him what he did after that town hall meeting. I can still see the clueless look on his face when he asked back, "What do you mean?" The fact that I had to explain my question was a huge indicator of the gap that existed. He had never communicated in any way to the entire group after the town hall meeting. What did he do now? His next hire was a communications director, and he amped up the frequency and type of communication in major ways and began the transformation of the engagement factor for his division.

Simon Sinek's TED Talk, "How Great Leaders Inspire Action"[4] is a great example of what we're talking about and is yet another framework for discussing vision. Just as I've outlined in this book the power and necessity of knowing our *Why*, Sinek amplifies the importance of this fact and indicates it's essential to be a successful leader. He speaks of Apple versus other technology companies and how their powerful *Why* has created unbelievable success. Sinek's video is another one of my go-to items in my coaching toolkit because I am astounded at how many leaders I've coached who haven't thought about their personal vision or the *Why* of their company, organization, or business unit. Or if they have, they haven't communicated it in a compelling and frequent manner.

I have referenced my role as president of TALX Corporation's largest division back in 2004. One of the key reasons we were able to achieve our level of success was that we helped the employees of that division, most of them from acquisitions, to see our vision and our *Why*, which helped them connect to the bigger vision of our company. When I took over as president, communication problems were rampant. What the employees were making up about our division was completely wrong, kept people from being engaged, and had them in fear of losing their jobs. One of the narratives people were telling was that we were going to sell off the division at some point, that the only reason they had been acquired was to access the data from their clients and once we had that, we would sell the division. Nothing could have been further from the truth, but the previous leader didn't have a vision, nor did he understand where we were going as a company. He had come from one of the acquisitions and had not bought into where we were going.

I found a clever example to help the leadership teams understand who we were. I used a Broadway play as a metaphor. At the time, Nathan Hale and Matthew Broderick were the two stars of the play *The Producers*. On the marquee of the theater was the name of the play and those two names, nothing else. We had another division that was the star of the company—one of the key reasons the investment community liked our company. What I explained to the people of our division was that, just like the play, there were probably 150 other people that it took to put on that play day after day, maybe more. But only two people got star billing. We were the 150 people behind the scenes, and if we did our job, took care of our clients, and grew our business, then the star division would achieve even more and better results, and we would all benefit by being part of a grow-ing, profitable company.

It helped them to see how they fit into the overall vision of the com-pany, why our division mattered, and more importantly, why each one of them mattered. I still have vivid memories of going to our seven offices around the US every quarter and standing before 50 or even 300 people and shouting, "Who's the most important division at TALX?"

And they would all scream, "We are!"

It was exhilarating for everyone, but especially for our leadership team because we could see that our employees understood and bought into the vision for our division.

Helen Keller had this to say about vision: "The only thing worse than being blind is having sight but no vision." A very powerful statement from someone who was blind but had a great vision for her life to the point that she understood its power.

At this point, if you've stopped and taken the time, or if you've already developed a vision, then it's time to think about how to communicate the vision to people who want and need to hear it. Remember, you must com-municate your vision *early* and *often* if you're leading a team, a department, or a company.

POINTS TO REMEMBER

- You can't deliver value unless you ground yourself in values.
- You must have a true north—a vision for yourself, your company, or your team.
- You can't communicate enough. If you think you're communicat-ing too much, keep communicating.
- You must know your *Why* if you are to be a successful leader.

CHAPTER 13

THE DIFFERENCE BETWEEN MISSION AND VISION STATEMENTS

The Vision is the public statement
of the founder's intent—
WHY the company exists.
It is literally the vision of a future that doesn't exist.
The Mission statement is a description
of the route, the guiding principles—
HOW the company intends to create that future.

—Simon Sinek

When we establish the mission that you, your department, or your company is on, we can explore the juncture of your values and your vision. Steven Covey says, "Fundamentally, your mission statement becomes your constitution, the solid expression of your vision and values. It becomes the criterion by which you measure everything else in your life."

Once we have our values and our vision identified, the mission statement can be easily developed by addressing the who, what, where, when, and why—our mission. Simply put, the difference between a mission statement and a vision statement is that a vision statement is typically aspirational and paints a view of the future, the north star that guides us personally, or guides our team, organization, or company to higher achievement. And once we have the vision, it becomes easier to determine the roadmap for how to get there.

The mission statement is about the here and now, what we do, possibly who we do it for, and it could include a statement of differentiation to our competitors or the market. Other elements could be placed in a mission statement, but it's important to first examine the fundamental difference between mission and vision. To better understand the difference here are some examples:

TED

Mission: Spread ideas.
Vision: We believe passionately in the power of ideas to change attitudes, lives, and ultimately, the world.

Tesla

Mission: To accelerate the world's transition to sustainable energy.
Vision: To create the most compelling car company of the 21st century by driving the world's transition to electric vehicles.

LinkedIn

Mission: To connect the world's professionals to make them more productive and successful.
Vision: To create economic opportunity for every member of the global workforce.

IKEA

Mission: Offer a wide range of well-designed, functional home furnishing products at prices so low that as many people as possible will be able to afford them.

Vision: To create a better everyday life for the many people of the world.

And here are my own mission and vision statements that I developed in the early 1990s and have continued to modify through the years to reflect changes in my own growth and development.

Ed Chaffin

Mission: To be an excellent, in-demand speaker, consultant, and executive coach and continue my learning to enhance my skills, knowledge, and expertise in order to excel in my own life and make a difference in the lives of people that I'm blessed to serve.

Vision: To change the world one life at a time by inspiring people, teams, and companies to be the best version of themselves.

Some areas to explore when developing your mission:
1. What impact do you want to have?
2. What do you want to change?
3. Who is the audience you want to serve?
4. How will you do what you want to do?
5. What is your competitive differentiation?

POINTS TO REMEMBER

- Our mission is the foundation laid upon our values.
- Our mission is the daily here and now of our vision for the future.

CHAPTER 14

TRUST, COMPASSION, STABILITY, AND HOPE

*Inner values like friendship, trust, honesty and compassion
are much more reliable than money—
they always bring happiness and strength.*

—Dalai Lama

The idea that vision is one of the most critical factors for leadership success may be contrary to the writings and beliefs of other alleged experts in the field of leadership development. As I previously mentioned, Gallup's writings have presented this disagreement. In an article published by Gallup in 2009, not long after the book *Strengths Based Leadership: Great Leaders, Teams, and Why People Follow*, by Tom Rath and Barry Conchie, they make the claim that vision "pales in comparison to instilling trust, compassion, stability, and hope."[1]

I contend that we have no reason or need to limit ourselves to an either/or debate. Life is complex and usually embraces a lot of both/and. So, once again I think this is a "yes, and" situation. If you have a grand vision for yourself, your team, division, or company, but you don't develop high levels of compassion, stability, and trust then yes, vision will pale.

Debating the value of vision versus trust and compassion is a bit like debating whether you need your right arm or your left arm. While we might favor one over the other, we all know it's best to have both.

In this New Reality where it is finally okay to admit that you're not okay, compassion for the diversity of responses and reactions has risen to a level we've never seen before. This is a sea change in the business world, and it brings about a philosophy of leadership that I've always had, and which I've referenced previously: *Who you are is how you lead. And who you are is the sum of everything that has happened to you since the day you were born (and maybe even when you were in the womb).* It is a myth of leadership that you can separate your personal life from your business life. We bring our "whole selves" into our work world each and every day.

We are all aware that trust is mission critical to leaders and followers, but it is an outcome of everything that you are doing as a leader. If you only focus on creating trust, then you may miss the nuances and the foundational elements that are necessary to create trust.

POINTS TO REMEMBER

- We need trust and compassion as well as vision. It's both/and.
- Who you are is how you lead.

LEADERSHIP REQUIRES 20/20 VISION

I referenced the restaurant and hospitality industries earlier. What is it about waiting tables, cooking in a kitchen, washing dishes, or ringing up sales in a retail establishment that leads someone to realize that they exist for a reason and should have a vision for their life? Or is it that jobs like these create the exact opposite effect? Whether or not bad bosses, rude customers, low pay, or stress are part of the picture, people realize they're in dead-end jobs going nowhere, and en masse they have decided to do something about it.

People are looking at their jobs in much clearer terms today. Does this align with who I am? Does this job support my goals and dreams? Or, very important right now, does this job provide positive mental health for me and my family? It's finally okay to not be okay and to talk about that fact. Open conversations about what we're dealing with as human beings have long been absent in the work world, but Covid changed that dynamic. And that is a great thing to have happened.

I don't have all the answers to explain what is going on, but as I talk to leaders, most are recognizing what is in the title of this book—we are in a New Reality. We may never go back to what used to be the standard workforce arrangements.

One key issue that I believe must be addressed is the disparity between what CEOs and top executives make in compensation on an annual basis versus the lowest-paid employee. I recognize that there are differences in responsibility, leadership value, and many other differences such as level of education and track record, but I'm not sure that fully explains the issue. In general, in the US, CEOs make about 300 times more than the average employee.[1] To express that another way, if I'm a CEO in the US, I make $18 million per year and you make $60,000. It's a ridiculous disparity. This book was not intended to dive deep into these two issues of the Great Resignation and executive compensation, but it occurred to me that as we address the New Reality, there are many subsets of issues that must be examined, and new solutions must appear for the workforces around the world.

After you've investigated your beliefs and your belief system, and explored your values, vision, and mission, the next building block is Principle #3: Leadership Is in the Eye of the Beholder. This third principle will be established on the strong foundation we've laid, and *the power is in the combination of the first two principles*—much like the concept of compound interest with money. There is a multiplier effect that is hard to quantify; at least that is what I believe. When we recognize and challenge our limiting beliefs, then rewrite those scripts, that in turn will allow us the freedom to investigate our *Why*—our values, vision and our mission for our life. When this compound interest effect kicks in, amazing changes and achievements become possible, and real, for each of us.

It's now time to step into your UnCommon Leadership® mantle. And you do that by recognizing this incredible fact about leadership: It's a full-time job and it's *personal*. You are never not leading! This also requires you to know who you are as a leader and how you affect others.

And it's *personalized*, meaning that what I want from my leaders may be very different than what they want.

The ideas and concepts you are about to read in the third section of the book are mission critical to leveraging what you've read, discovered, and hopefully implemented in the first two sections.

The third section will provide a deeper understanding of two wise imperatives—know thyself and seek first to understand. We will then look at how those maxims can create trust, compassion, stability, and hope!

PRINCIPLE 3

LEADERSHIP IS IN THE EYE OF THE BEHOLDER

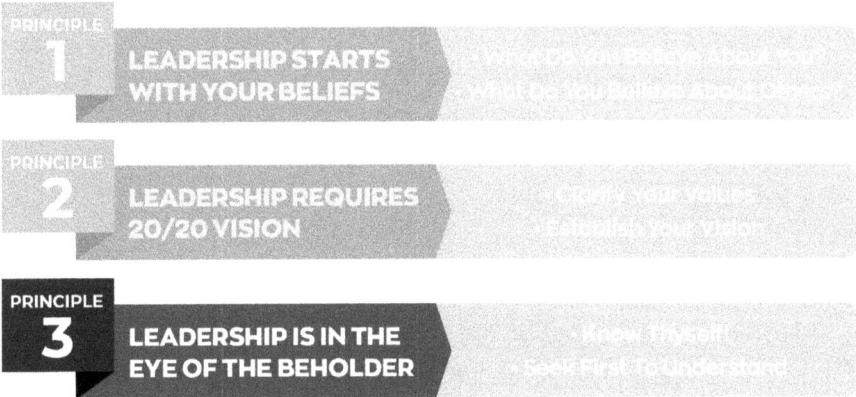

PRINCIPLE 1

LEADERSHIP STARTS WITH YOUR BELIEFS
- What Do You Believe About You?
- What Do You Believe About Others?

PRINCIPLE 2

LEADERSHIP REQUIRES 20/20 VISION
- Clarify Your Values
- Establish Your Vision

PRINCIPLE 3

LEADERSHIP IS IN THE EYE OF THE BEHOLDER
- Know Thyself!
- Seek First To Understand

CHAPTER 15

LEADERSHIP REQUIRES NEW THINKING FOR THE NEW REALITY

Most of us just "do" what we do as leaders without realizing how we affect others with our natural leadership styles.

—Ed Chaffin

Never has it been more necessary to embrace the ethos of this last principle—Leadership is in the eye of the beholder.

Using the 1-to-99 scale that I mentioned earlier when discussing change, in relation to the post-Covid New Reality, the people scoring 1 on the scale have struggled mightily with the significant changes that have been forced on them, and the 99s are saying, "This is great! Bring on some more change!" Then there's everyone else somewhere in between, and they all potentially see this situation very differently—but definitely from their own personal viewpoint and perceptions. We as leaders can no longer assume that we fully understand the intrinsic motivations and needs of the people we lead, including ourselves! I don't know anyone who hasn't had to do some level of reset in their lives, and in some cases make radical changes to the way they live, work, and play. This is the essence of this book, and it's one of the key factors in the Great Resignation.

As with all challenges we face, there are positive takeaways if we adjust our mindset and ask ourselves good questions. One positive is that people want their voices to be heard, and they aren't being bashful about it. Some leaders may fear this newfound voice of their staff, but if they avoid it, they will miss the opportunity to reinvent how they lead, and they will not find new ways to apply human-centered leadership models. If they don't find new leadership models, this new life and energy we see in employees' efforts to take charge of their lives and careers will continue to lead to mass defections in the workforce.

And here's the data that backs this up: Depending on the source, anywhere from 46 to 95 percent of employees say they are going to make a career and/or job change.

As leaders, the vast spectrum of perceptions, beliefs, and attitudes represented by this span of responses presents both challenges and opportunities to recognize the need for a drastic shift in how we approach our leadership mantle.

If you think about yourself as a follower, haven't you experienced situations where one-size-fits-all leadership either worked for you or it didn't? Or maybe the extreme is that the leader's usual style isn't working for anyone, but the leader doesn't care and isn't motivated to realize that a shift is necessary to bring out the best in the people they're leading. I've been called to coach quite a few leaders in different companies who were told, "Shape up or ship out!"

Leadership is personal and can be driven by our perceptions or our misperceptions. A good example of this is from a while back when a viral image of a dress hit the internet. Some saw it as only gold and white, while others saw black and blue. I use that image when I do talks or team programs for leadership teams, and it's amazing the divergence in what people see. I've never been able to see black and blue, and I just don't understand how people can see those colors.

In one case, I was the only person in the room of 15 people who saw white and gold. They all thought I was from the planet Mars and couldn't understand how I could not see the black and blue colors they were seeing.

One person even walked up to the screen and pointed to each area. "Ed, see this area? It's blue. Look hard and you'll see blue!" No, I couldn't! He was truly baffled. This is an example of the fact that your eyes and your brain work together to make sense of things you experience, and they produce different images for different people.

This is a vivid example of how you and I can experience the exact same event, see the exact same thing, and come away with very different opinions of what we experienced or saw.

Here's another example I use when I do a talk. How many times have you attended a meeting with a team of people, then walked out of the meeting, and in your discussion with someone who was also in that same meeting, you realize that each of you both had different opinions about what was discussed or what was decided? This happens quite often.

These two examples show us what I described in detail in the first section—that because the brain doesn't know fact from fiction, we can develop different perceptions and misperceptions. When we experience people or events, we develop "stories" that help us make sense of what we are experiencing. And these stories lead us to create our version of reality that may not be a reality to someone else.

Another phenomenon is that of *time and distance*. The more time and distance removes us from an event, the more distorted our stories and beliefs can be about what happened. It's called the conflating of events because we can integrate separate events or experiences and begin to think they were the same. This happened with the reporter Brian Williams of NBC in relation to an incident in Iraq in 2003 in which a military helicopter took fire and was forced to land. Over time, he became convinced that he was actually in the helicopter that got shot at versus being in a trailing copter that witnessed the event.

The point is this: *You* are in control of what you believe about yourself, and you may or may not have an accurate view of yourself. And you may especially not have an accurate view of others. These beliefs about yourself and others drive what type of leader inspires and motivates you.

Like the survey respondents on that 1-to-99 scale, some of us want our leader to be firm and in control and even give us detailed directions. Others of us want our leader to give us the high-level goal and then let us figure out how to get it done. Each of us can have a very different version of what a great leader is or what makes a great leader.

When I have performed speeches or workshops and discussed this topic of leadership being in the eye of the beholder I ask the audience if they can provide a one-word definition of leadership. I'll get responses like "visionary," "authentic," "charismatic," "trustworthy," and many more. Barry Posner and Jim Kouzes, authors of *The Leadership Challenge* I referenced in the second section, have been asking that question for more than 30 years. What is the one word they believe defines leadership? *Relationships.*

If people don't know you care, they probably don't care about you as their leader. This section is about the resulting challenge—each of us may define leadership differently, which means we each want something different from our leaders.

POINTS TO REMEMBER

- Each of us has our own view and opinion of what great leadership is.
- We can experience the same event and come away with completely different versions of the event.

CHAPTER 16

THE SOCK-SOCK, SHOE-SHOE STORY

We are what we repeatedly do.
Excellence, then, is not an act, but a habit.

—Aristotle

This third section could have been titled "You're Never Not Leading," which would have indicated the direction as well. The double negative is like the boss who says nothing, but everyone knows not to approach him that day. First we'll explore the fact that so much of what we do is in what I have deemed to be in *"automagic" mode.* I created that word as I believe it best describes how so much of what we do is on autopilot!

Brain scientists estimate that on any given day we do 95 to 99 percent of what we do, including making decisions, on automagic mode.[1]

We are not cognitively engaging our brain each and every time we do something. This is the brain's way of creating efficiency, because if we had to think in detail about everything we did and think about every decision we made, it would burn up the glycogen in our brains necessary for cognitive function.

Because the brain must have efficiency, it creates huge neural pathways that drive this automagic mode we operate in. The leadership truth related to this brain fact is that many of us do what we do without deep thought into our intentions and the effect we have on the people we lead.

I already mentioned the phrase, "If you keep doing what you're doing, you'll keep getting what you've always gotten." And as we just learned, so much of what we're doing we may not even be fully aware of.

Socrates famously said, "The unexamined life is not worth living." How do you examine your life (and your leadership)? Start with sock-sock, shoe-shoe! Let me illustrate this with a story from a seven-year-old.

One Sunday morning I was helping my then seven-year-old daughter get dressed for church. I was hurrying around on autopilot when she jumped on the bed in her pretty dress, and I stopped to help her put on her little, black, patent leather shoes. As I was buckling the first strap, in her high, little voice, she piped up and asked me a profound question. "Daddy, when you get dressed, do you put on sock-sock, shoe-shoe? Or do you put on sock-shoe, sock-shoe?"

I was stunned. I sat down on the bed, looked her in the eye, and said, "Erica, I honestly don't know. I have to think about it." When I did think about it, I told her I did sock-sock, shoe-shoe, lace-lace because on that day I wore shoes with laces.

She proudly stated, "I put on sock-shoe, sock-shoe."

What happened in that short exchange?

My daughter forced me to *stop* and *think* about a routine task that I do most days unless I decide to run around barefoot. I had *never* once thought about how I put on my shoes. Have you? Probably not. The reason? What I stated earlier—our brains do 95 to 99 percent of everything we do on autopilot.

This is a challenge for most of us. We either do not or will not stop and think about the things we do every day, how we are showing up, and how we are leading. How many of the automagic things we do empower us or help us achieve our goals? Or how many of them move us toward being great leaders?

Don't get me wrong. A lot of the automagic stuff we do is great, like breathing, for example. But how much do we do that we don't even realize, and how much of that is productive, intentional, and connected to what we want to change, grow, or achieve?

When you put your shoes on, is it sock-sock, shoe-shoe? Or sock-shoe, sock-shoe? Let's go further. Which sock do you start with, left or right? It's startling how much we do without thinking! So it is with our natural leadership style. We may have no idea how we really lead and how we affect others in the way we show up and lead.

I've told the above story many times in workshops, seminars, and speeches. And I've received some great reactions. Recently, I ran into someone who had been at one of my workshops, and he said, "Damn you, Ed Chaffin! I can't get dressed in the morning now without thinking about my socks and shoes and you!"

I said, "You're welcome!" You can see the point of that comment. He was made aware of his awareness. And once you become aware of your awareness, you can't go back to being unaware. This can be a wonderful thing if you begin to prioritize what you think about.

If you think about this story from the perspective of change, it can create a shift for us to realize why so many of our efforts to change things in our life don't happen. We run our beliefs and scripts on autopilot without ever stopping to determine if they're working or not. Our efforts at changing organizations, teams, or any group of people require sometimes herculean efforts to drive the change that is needed.

You are always leading, and let's repeat for emphasis, *you're never not leading*. This is the number-one piece of feedback I've received from leaders and executives I've coached: "I never realized this before, that everything I'm thinking, doing, and saying is being observed, and it's being absorbed by the people around me." So how are you showing up, and what are you bringing into the office or the Zoom call? All of these things are related to the *person effect* that I referenced earlier in the book, how we affect others.

Think about meeting someone for the first time, and for some unknown reason you just don't like that person. The opposite is equally true in that you may be instantly attracted to them and think they could become a best friend or that you would like to work with them.

It is important to understand this energy concept and connect it to how you show up and how you lead, especially in these epic times in which we now live. People are hungering for leaders who can adapt their leadership to the situation and the person. We must question if how we normally lead is working for the people we lead. My guess is that a great number of people have never examined at a deep level who they are as a leader and what their default leadership style(s) may be.

We'll continue to explore the critical elements to establishing ourselves as the kind of leader people want to follow. My belief is that you will gain a new awareness of your own personal leadership and understand the truth that leadership is in the eye of the beholder.

POINTS TO REMEMBER

- Our brains like efficiency. Therefore, we do many things without actually thinking about what or how we are doing them—including leadership.
- You have an effect on everyone you meet or experience. Do you know what that is?

CHAPTER 17

YOUR PRESENCE AND YOUR ENERGY MATTER

What you do speaks so loudly
that I can't hear what you're saying.

—Ralph Waldo Emerson

As Emerson states, so it is with our brains, which are wanting to make sense of events and experiences. When you show up, your whole person shows up each and every time, and it's not just your words that affect others, it's the entire essence of you—including your energy. You and I produce energy fields that emanate from our bodies and our brains, whether we want it to happen or not. Earlier I referenced Dawson Church's *Mind to Matter: The Astonishing Science of How Your Brain Creates Material Reality.* Church has quantified for us the way that we produce these energy fields. What we now know is that you and I put out an energy field with a radius of about 15 feet and when we are about 5 feet away from each other, our brains are communicating subconsciously to figure out if we like and can trust each other.[1] This all happens in the background in nanoseconds. Which is why understanding basic brain-based leadership is important, and it may be a new concept for some. We aren't consciously aware of this energy exchange and in some cases not aware of the impact we are having on others. Brain-based leadership is foundational to developing your self-leadership and leading others.

This is one of the reasons we see so many diverse effects of, and reactions to, our New Reality. Most of us now spend our days on web-based calls, and our brains are working overtime to figure out what they used to be able to do on autopilot when we were in close contact. It's just not the same human interaction that we have used for millennia to relate with other human beings and one of the key factors is the stress that these meetings are creating. In a *Forbes* article titled "Our Brains Need Breaks From Virtual Meetings" the author cites a Microsoft study conducted by their Human Factors Lab that measured the brain waves of people attending virtual meetings. They provided the following key results:

1. Breaks between meetings allow the brain to "reset," reducing the cumulative build-up of stress.
2. Back-to-back meetings can decrease your ability to focus and engage.
3. Transitioning between meetings can be a source of high stress.[2]

Zoom/Teams fatigue is a real thing, and a large part of our population around the world is struggling with it. We've replaced quick chats at the water cooler or coffee machine with a near-constant stream of web meetings. Even well-intentioned initiatives to eliminate Zoom calls on Fridays can have the opposite effect. They create a jam-packed Monday through Thursday that leaves us exhausted by Friday. One idea has been to create web-based meetings where everyone just turns off their cameras. This harkens back to the conference call days, so why don't we just go back to that method more often? Oh, I forgot. We *must* have the chat feature to communicate in another way during those meetings, so we can't just be on a conference call. God forbid that we would not be able to text/chat for 30 minutes to an hour!

The key to understanding our current dilemma is this: *Leadership is energy—your energy*. It starts, and it ends, with how you show up and what you are putting out. Here's an example most of us can relate to. Have you ever been warned about not approaching the boss today about your great idea or the promotion that you believe is overdue or that raise you were promised last quarter? Or someone said to you as you arrived at work, or texted you just as you arrived on the Zoom call, "Be careful with John today. He isn't in a good mood"?

If you ask them how they know John isn't in a good mood, most often they'll say something like, "You can just tell," or, "I just know," or, "You can see it in his face." The boss may not have said a word, but the energy he's putting out says, *Stay away. Don't mess with me today.*

The flip side to this is that when we recognize that leadership starts with our energy, we can make conscious choices about how we show up, especially if we know and understand that our energy is contagious. What I put out will often come back to me in the form of people who either become enthused by my energy or become depressed because of it. If you think about that dynamic, you realize the incredible power you possess as a leader simply by how you exhibit your body language, word choices, the volume and tone of your voice, and that mysterious, invisible energy that emanates from your being. This is one of the reasons many people subscribe to the false belief that to be a great leader, you need to have charisma or that "it" factor. Yes, having great energy, motivating people by excitement and enthusiasm, and marshaling the troops toward turning a vision into reality is a key factor. But there must be some substance behind the charisma, or you're nothing more than a carnival barker—and definitely not an UnCommon Leader.

From the executive coaching work and team development I've been doing for many years, I've seen that most people just show up and do what they do. We're not thinking about the fact that, no matter what, we are *always* leading, and most of us are on automagic mode. We are not intentional about recognizing the incredible power we possess by our presence.

This brings us to the question: Do you really understand who you are as a leader, what your default leadership style(s) are, and how you affect others with the way you lead? The imperative for each of us is to follow Socrates' dictum that the unexamined life is not worth living and examine our lives to understand ourselves at a much deeper level than most of us have done. And in this self-examination, we give special attention to how we show up and lead.

We think we know who we are. We think we are self-aware. But as my good friend Terry Small, a.k.a. The Brain Guy likes to say, "It's hard to read the label when you're inside the bottle!" Even when we think we know who we are, we must be honest enough to recognize what Terry is saying. We have perceptions of ourselves that can also be misperceptions. And these misperceptions can create a path for us that doesn't align with current reality, or with our dreams and goals, or with who we want to be as a leader.

Here is another personal story that amplifies Emerson's quote, "What you do speaks so loudly that I can't hear what you're saying." It is a bit painful to tell because it illustrates the dilemma of how to have an accurate view of who we are and how we affect others with our natural leadership style.

This was a pivotal moment in my leadership development, and it took someone's willingness to "speak truth to power" for me to see that I did not have an accurate view of myself. And it came from a 12-year-old, the same daughter who at 7 woke me up with the sock-sock, shoe-shoe question.

I was having a conversation with Erica, and at one point she said, "Dad, stop yelling." My immediate reaction was, "I'm not yelling. I'm just making a point."

To her credit, she didn't back down and came right back with, "Yes, you are yelling at me."

My knee-jerk reaction was to tell her one more time that I wasn't yelling, but something stopped me. I'm not sure what it was, but I believe it was because I heard the sincerity in her voice, and I saw in her body language that my method of talking to her wasn't aligning with who she was and what she wanted in her leader, specifically in her dad.

So I asked her, "What makes the way I'm talking seem like I'm yelling at you?" She described the intensity of my voice, my aggressive body language, and how it was "landing" on her as not being very kind. I was being forceful in my effort to get her to understand something.

This was a huge wake-up call for me. At that point I had been on a ten-year journey of a total reinvention of who I was as a person, son, father, husband, and leader. I had made tremendous progress, but somehow I had missed something very important to a very important person in my life.

Without that interaction, I'm not sure I would have learned that my natural communication style could be considered intense or aggressive to some people. It was from this experience that I learned I had a faulty belief system around communications. I thought I was a great communicator to everyone because I had spent time starting and building Toastmasters chapters, had participated in speech contests, and had developed what I thought was a great ability to speak and communicate. But speaking to an audience is *very* different from one-to-one communication or communicating to your team of ten people, and I had missed the mark.

In my one-to-one interactions, there was still a big component missing—understanding what that audience wanted and needed from me, and that my natural leadership and communication style affected different people in very different ways. Another way of saying this is that I was missing the fact that, no matter what, I was always leading, and the way I was leading might or might not work at certain times or with certain people.

This was one of my first major insights into the model of personal and personalized leadership I developed over the past 25 years that drove the writing of this book. It also connects to the title of this section. Up until that point with my daughter, I did what a lot of people do. I simply led without any consideration for whether I was connecting with the deepest intrinsic motivations of the people I was communicating with and leading.

POINTS TO REMEMBER

- Whether you want to or not, you are *always* leading.
- You create energy with your presence—get intentional about putting out positive energy.

CHAPTER 18

READING THE LABEL—HOW DO WE REALLY KNOW HOW WE LEAD?

If we give people enough cheese then we think they'll move.
But people are more complex than lab rats.
Intrinsic motivation, coming from within, is a powerful thing.

—Dan Ariely

It's extremely important to understand what drives you—who you are as a person and as a leader—and what your default leadership style(s) may be. Most of us have heard that we should be life-long learners. But my question to you is, how much of your life-long learning has focused on that deep examination of exactly who you are as a person and a leader?

How do we get an accurate picture of who we are as a leader? Back to Terry Small's quote that "It's hard to read the label when you're inside the bottle," it is a challenge to fully understand and comprehend how you affect others and whether it's working for the people you are fortunate enough to lead. Three methods could enable you to accomplish this.

METHOD ONE

First, invite others into your growth and development. It may be the best way to gain that honest feedback of who you are and how you affect others with your natural leadership style, as my daughter did regarding my "yelling." That was uninvited, but it was a powerful exchange, and it altered my perspective about how I was leading.

Inviting others into your leadership journey can be very challenging, but it is crucial. I had a CEO coaching client, and we did a 180-degree qualitative review in which I only talked to her direct reports. Some of the feedback wasn't very positive. I had to give her space to sort through the information as it was tough to hear how she was missing as a leader in the eyes of some of her direct reports. However, the critical factor of the feedback was that it was all over the board. One person thought she was an incredible leader and met all their needs, and the next one was ready to walk out the door because of the poor leadership they experienced.

Years earlier I myself had learned this kind of thing in a big way—back in the time I described in the introduction when I became president of my former company's largest division. About six months into the new role, I hired an executive coach to perform both a quantitative and qualitative 360-degree evaluation to see how I was doing in this new, challenging role and what, if anything needed adjusting in my leadership style. The qualitative part of the project required my executive coach to interview my boss and my peers as well as my direct reports. My personal view at that time was that I thought I was doing an incredible job of leading the division. The energy and excitement on our team were palpable, and I didn't think there was anything that I would need to radically change. I couldn't have been more wrong.

I remember the conversation with my executive coach, Kathy, as if it were yesterday. She had a unique way of presenting the information based on brain-based leadership. She presented five things I was doing well and how they drove the team and the division to new heights. My number-one positive attribute was creating and painting a clear vision for our division. And I was glowing by the time she got to number five.

Then Kathy dropped the hammer when she presented the *one* thing that had to change. It seemed that my enthusiasm, energy, and passion had created a tsunami of excitement about where we were going and how we would achieve success, but all that energy and passion had created a pace of action on a day-to-day basis that was producing exhaustion from some of my direct reports.

She said, "Ed, you're running and moving so fast that you haven't taken the time to turn around and see who can keep up with you. They all are trying their best, but not every one of them can run at your pace. You must make some adjustments in your leadership to allow those who need more time to accept change, make big decisions, and come up with creative solutions to do just that."

Most of us have a dominant leadership or communication style and possibly another style that we can activate when required. My default leadership style could be labeled as pacesetting, and I firmly believe it was the right style at the time. When I took over as president, we had accomplished four acquisitions within the unemployment space and were investigating a possible fifth. The people who had come from the first four companies didn't understand where we were going and the *why* of our division, so there was a sense of urgency to get everyone on the same page as quickly as possible. While the pace-setting style was needed to help blend many cultures into one, I wasn't aware of the person effect I was having on some of my team in that they wanted to keep up but simply couldn't.

Here's the valuable thing to know: I already had the data to know this information, but I hadn't taken the time to apply it in a meaningful manner. That was another wake-up call for me, and it radically changed who I was as a leader. This was the beginning for me to truly understand what personal and personalized leadership (UnCommon Leadership®) meant and how to put it into action.

Kathy Cramer was not only my executive coach but the founder of The Kramer Institute that had performed the 360. We hired Kathy to come and bring in some of her thinking to our division. She was incredible and helped us elevate our leadership and vision for our division. She wrote several books around the topic of changing the way you see things. Unfortunately, Kathy passed away a few years ago after a battle with cancer, but her legacy lives on in me and my leadership due to the profound impact she had on me as a person and as a leader. I will always be deeply indebted to her for what she did for me, for our leadership team, and our division.

If hiring a coach and performing a 180 or 360 is not possible, then what can you do? This leads to the next suggestion.

METHOD TWO

Second, directly ask the people you're leading. I often hear from C-suite leaders that it is hard to get direct, actionable feedback. But my encouragement is that if you approach this using the coaching style of leadership—which is to ask great questions and listen to learn, not to respond—then you can probably have some success.

When it's time for your next one-to-one meeting you might consider asking the following questions:

1. When we work together, what about my style of leadership works well for you?
2. What else?
3. What about my leadership style would you like to see me do differently?
4. What else?
5. What about my leadership style works well for the team?
6. What else?
7. What about my leadership style could change to create more effectiveness for the team?
8. What else?

Note the repetition of the question, "What else?" In my coaching work, I've discovered that the first answer to a question can often be superficial, and it requires asking "what else" to keep their brains in the search mode for more and deeper answers. You might even consider asking "What else?" more than once.

Almost always there is "something else," and if you continue to direct their brains to think that way, you'll often gain valuable insight. This is because your brain is a very powerful endless loop computer, and if you keep asking it great questions, it will keep searching to find great answers.

I'm sure if you think about it, you can come up with other questions that may be more specific to your business unit or team. For example, on a specific project being run by team members who are mission-critical to the success of the business unit or the company, you could generate direct questions about how you as the leader are managing and holding people accountable for the success of the project.

You must find out how you affect people with your natural leadership style as well as identify which leadership style or styles are your dominant or default style and which you should focus on growing and developing more. Most of us are probably using just one style most of the time, and it may or may not be the right style for the moment, the team, or the person.

METHOD THREE

Third, a good method for discovering who you are as a leader and how you affect others is to use assessments. There are thousands of them for you to choose from, and I encourage you to choose carefully. Not all assessments will provide what you need. Why? Because most ask you questions about yourself. What have we already learned? That it's hard to read the label when you're inside the bottle! What is my go-to assessment that I've trusted for decades? The Birkman Method® assessment, which I referenced in the introduction. When I received the feedback from my coach about what I needed to change, I gained the exact information I needed to know how to adjust my leadership style to tap into the needs of each person, versus a one-size-fits-all method of leading that I had been using. I'll cover the Birkman Method in more detail later in this section, but for now, let's keep exploring the person effect and the brain-based leadership connection.

POINTS TO REMEMBER

- It is critical to understand how you lead and how others experience you.
- Most people have one or two dominant leadership styles. Do you know what they are?

CHAPTER 19

BRAIN-BASED LEADERSHIP—PSYCHOLOGICAL SAFETY DRIVES CONNECTIVITY

*Psychological safety is a belief that one will
not be punished or humiliated for speaking up
with ideas, questions, concerns, or mistakes,
and that the team is safe for interpersonal risk-taking.*

—Amy Edmondson

When we recognize that the brain's number one job is to keep you alive and safe, we must also realize that it will lie to you if it means keeping you alive. For vivid examples of how your brain works, I refer again to the program *Brain Games* that was once on the National Geographic channel. If you can find it online, I encourage you to watch a few episodes. You'll discover in greater depth this discussion about your brain's not knowing fact from fiction.

Because of this key role of our brain, it is imperative that we understand how powerful of a driver this can be in regard to our own personal leadership.

Many of us in leadership roles have heard of the study Google performed with its "Project Aristotle."[1] They sought to discover the factors that led to high-performing teams with high productivity and an abundance of trust. They found five key factors: impact, meaning, structure and clarity, dependability, and the number-one factor of psychological safety.

1 PSYCHOLOGICAL SAFETY
Team members feel safe to take risks and be vulnerable in front of each other.

2 DEPENDABILITY
Team members get things done on time and meet Google's high bar for excellence.

3 STRUCTURE & CLARITY
Team members have clear roles, plans, and goals.

4 MEANING
Work is personally important to team members.

5 IMPACT
Team members think their work matters and creates change.

What does psychological safety mean? It means that a high level of trust has been created, and team members feel safe to take risks and be vulnerable with each other. For leaders, this means that your number-one job as a leader is to create this same level of safety on your team. You must help the people you lead turn off the negative biases they naturally have.

The number-one job of the brain is to keep you alive and safe. That's the evolutionary process we have arrived at, and the importance of this cannot be overstated because it impacts leadership.

We are descendants not of Betty and Barney Rubble, who came out of the cave in the morning and said things like, "Look at the sky, how blue it is! And look at the flowers blooming. They're so beautiful!" Those ancestors were eaten. We are the ancestors of Fred and Wilma Flintstone, who came out and looked around to see if there was danger. Fred would put his ear on the ground to sense if there were thundering footsteps of the Tyrannosaurus Rex. And if he did, he'd run back into the cave to live another day.[2] Your brain is hard-wired to keep you alive and safe, so it has a naturally guarded, or negative, bias. It's constantly scanning the environment to determine if danger is lurking. Imagine that you're back in the office, and you walk up to the doorway of one of your direct reports. Their brain is immediately trying to determine if you're going to eat them or love them. And it's doing so subconsciously in a nano-second.

We have this baseline of understanding now that our brains have a negative bias, but this conversation has yet another level. I have a certification in brain-based leadership from The Academy of Brain-based Leadership (ABL) located in Southern California, and their model takes the concept of psychological safety to the personal level. That can be approached by asking, "How do each of us define psychological safety?"

If you have a team of ten people who report to you, and you simply say that psychological safety is what we all need, that's not enough because each of us may define safety differently. Like our values conversation in the second section, how you define something may be different from someone else, and that difference could be stark.

ABL uses a model based on five domains they believe are important to each of us on a one-to-ten scale: Security, Autonomy, Fairness, Esteem, and Trust. They add a *Y* for You to form the acronym, S.A.F.E.T.Y.[3] And that's what we want to create in our companies, business units, and teams—an environment where it's safe to take risks, explore, and not worry about success or failure.

Some companies that create awareness around these S.A.F.E.T.Y elements realize the value of celebrating failure, like Intuit, the tax software company. Co-founder Scott Cook says, "At Intuit we celebrate failure because every failure teaches something important that can be seen for the next great idea." And they back up their commitment to celebrating failure by giving a special award for the Best Failure and actually conduct failure parties![4] This aligns with the story I told of my former CEO telling me that if it didn't work out for my running our largest division, he would find a place for me. I was free to go do what he had asked me to do and not worry about success or failure.

Here are the definitions of the ABL S.A.F.E.T.Y.™ Model:

Security. Security is the brain's need for predictability. It is all about the C's in the environment. The brain likes consistency, commitment, clarity, certainty, and dislikes change; these all go a long way to making the brain feel that its environment is safe.

Autonomy. Autonomy is the feeling of control over one's environment, whether the control is real or not. A sensation of having choices within any given situation is rewarding to the brain. Let's face it, few of us like to be told what to do. Lack of control, powerlessness, or helplessness have a major impact on our health and blood pressure.

Fairness. We want exchanges that occur within our environment to be fair to us and to others. Fair exchanges are intrinsically rewarding, independent of other factors. When something is seen as unfair, the brain deals with it using the same networks as those involved with disgust.

Esteem. This domain covers the topics of how we view ourselves, how we compare ourselves with others, and how we think others view us. Research indicates that having a positive view of ourselves adds to our health and general well-being.

Trust. This domain addresses our social needs. We thrive in tribes; initially however, we treat each new person as a stranger or threat. They are part of our out-group. As we establish commonalities, they become part of our in-group, and we now use a different brain network to deal with them.

You. The impact of this domain can be so strong that it can outweigh any or all of the previous five. Some of the aspects that can impact this domain are your personality, your biases, patterns, habits and triggers, your past experiences, your future plans, your current situation, and your future outlook.[5]

As I was going through the certification process with ABL, I completed their assessment of the S.A.F.E.T.Y. model and found that my top two elements were Autonomy and Trust. As you read the definitions, you may have seen one or two that stood out for you, and without taking the assessment you know intuitively that it's *the* most important one for you. However, while it's a worthwhile exercise, realize that our intuition is subject to our biases and blind spots that we have about ourselves, so the assessment serves to somewhat mitigate those blind spots by providing a more objective way of discovering both the most important elements and the magnitude of importance you place on them compared to the thousands of people who have taken the assessment.

As you read the definitions you possibly thought of someone else whom you suspect might have a very different profile. For example, someone who would have the opposite of my Autonomy element would have Security as their number-one factor. Can you imagine the different perspectives each of us would bring to a team that was striving for peak performance? I want to be free from constraints, be able to work on my own, and possibly take more risks. The person with Security as their top element might be averse to taking risks. Could we work together? Yes, but there would be challenges if we didn't respect and value those differences and create the language and dialogue to have healthy conversations when our working together created stress for one another.

The point is to recognize that each of us may have a different profile and have different elements that are the most important. It's not enough to recognize that as a leader we want and need to create an environment where people feel safe and create trust. This is what I referred to earlier in that trust is an outcome. We also need to know what the most important factors are for each person because it's an individual thing. It's personalized leadership.

If you can't take ABL's assessment and have your team take it, then what can you do to learn what is important to each team member?

It begins with a mindset shift in you as a leader toward being motivated to care about people at a more personal level. You must show them that you care about them first and foremost as people and not just the results they bring to the team or the company. As I referenced earlier in describing how to know how you are affecting others with your leadership style you must become a leader who asks great questions. This is fundamental to finding out how to lead each of your team members in a manner that drives their intrinsic motivations and unleashes their creativity and personal power. Another important component of this process is that you must become a great listener as well. St. Francis of Assisi said, "Seek first to understand before trying to be understood." This is the major shift so many of us leaders should make—from being advocates for our ideas and positions to becoming much more curious about the wants, needs, and ideas of other people on the team.

You can show them you care by getting to know them and by asking great questions and listening intently to their responses. Here are some questions to consider:

1. Tell me about the best leader that you've ever worked for (besides me!).
2. What made them a great leader?
3. What's important to you about the work you do here?
4. What could I do as your leader that would empower you more?
5. Has there ever been a time when you didn't feel valued?
6. If so, what made you feel devalued?
7. Has there been a time when you felt highly valued working on this team?
8. If so, what made you feel highly valued?

I can't overemphasize how powerful a shift this can be for most leaders because so many of us have arrived at our level of leadership because we are solution-oriented, know how to advocate for our ideas, and get things done. And a major way that we do that is by telling people what to do or where we're going and talking at them—versus gaining their perspective and perceptions by truly listening to what they are saying and becoming much more curious about other people and what they need from their leaders. For me it's one of the main differences between managing and leading. You recognize that you don't have all the answers, and you want to tap into the collective intelligence of your team members—versus thinking you always have all the answers. Remember, the sum of all of us is better than any one of us!

In the current work environment, you can't have too many of these one-to-one conversations with your team members. You must not leave this to chance as so many of us do. But fortunately, there are two parts of our brain, the hardware and the software. The hardware is the gray matter of neural networks. The software we call the mind's eye, where with intentional focus, effort, desire, passion, vision, and goals, we can design what it looks like to play to win for ourselves and others.

POINTS TO REMEMBER

- Psychological safety is personal. And we can differ in how we believe it's created.
- Seek first to understand before being understood.

CHAPTER 20

HOW MUCH SHOULD A LEADER CARE?

Beginning today, treat everyone you meet
as if they were going to be dead by midnight.
Extend to them all the care, kindness and understanding
you can muster and do it with no thought of any reward.
Your life will never be the same again.

—Og Mandino

As a leader, you must show that you care about people at a personal level, and that is foundational to developing high levels of trust. As I mentioned previously, I was privileged to coach at The Institute of Management and Development (IMD) in Lausanne, Switzerland for almost ten years in the High Performance Leadership executive development program led by IMD's professor of leadership, Dr. George Kohlrieser.

It is, and has been, the number-one open enrollment program at IMD for many years. Dr. Kohlrieser developed a model of leadership based on the research of the noted evolutionary psychologist Dr. John Bowlby, as well as developmental psychologist Dr. Mary Ainsworth, and many others. Both Bowlby and Ainsworth are known for researching, studying, and developing the concept of attachment theory, and from the best research I can find, both were some of the first researchers to use the term "secure base" in describing the positives that come from someone creating strong attachments with people who are important to them in their lives.[1]

Bowlby described a secure base and its psychological effects this way: "When an individual is confident that an attachment figure will be available to him whenever he desires it, that person will be much less prone to either intense or chronic fear than will an individual who for any reason has no such confidence."[2] What this accomplishes is that it frees the person to take risks and seek adventure.

Kohlrieser developed and taught the concept of secure base leadership, referenced first in his book *Hostage at the Table*[3] and then codified in more detail in his second book, *Care To Dare*,[4] written with co-authors Susan Goldsworthy and Duncan Coombe. His is a model that requires you as the leader to become a secure base for the people whom you're leading. In doing so, you can turn off the natural, negative bias of people's brains, or as stated before, create psychological safety for those around you and those that you lead. And if we are to be secure bases for those we lead, then we must have secure bases in our lives, and those secure bases can go beyond a person. They can be events such as my bike race story you read earlier, or the marathon that I ran. Both of those events provided an "attachment" for me that showed me that I could accomplish something that previously I didn't think possible. That has allowed me to stretch and go beyond perceived limitations in many other areas of my life.

There can be many forms of secure bases. They can be places like the beach or the mountains. They can be symbols or even objects. When my father died in 1999 my mother gave me his wedding band. I've worn it ever since and it provides a connection to someone that was important to me.

Your faith in a deity or the book of that faith such as the Bible or the Koran can be a secure base. I think that you get the picture that secure bases can take many forms, and they all accomplish the same goal—allowing us to be free to explore, stretch, and grow.

One final comment: We also must be secure bases for ourselves. As I've just shown, secure bases go beyond "attachment figures," and these extensions then move to you becoming your own secure base. I believe that the information that you've read in this book has provided a strong foundation for you to examine who you are and where you are going, and when you do the work that's been prescribed so far, you can begin to build the confidence in yourself to trust yourself more. Trusting yourself and having the confidence to step into your UnCommon Leadership mantle is an imperative, and that confidence (not arrogance) can create an environment that unleashes high productivity and creativity, and allows the people you are leading to take risks.

The model presented by Kohlrieser, Goldsworthy, and Coombe is called *Caring and Daring*. When we as leaders create an environment where we are bonded at a deep level that has created trust, then we have earned the right to dare others to be a better version of themselves. If we don't, then it's possible that we are allowing people to not stretch and grow and even enabling them to be less than they could be.

A similar model comes from the book *Radical Candor* by Kim Scott.[5] In her model, once we establish that we are secure bases and create a caring relationship with those we lead, then we have earned the opportunity to challenge them to be the best version of themselves. Scott calls it *Caring and Challenging*, as you can see in the diagram below. Kohlrieser's model of "Caring and Daring" is the same. I encourage you to read both books, especially *Hostage at The Table*, as Kohlrieser also explores a topic that is so relevant in today's times—loss and grief. Here's the point: You as a leader should care 100 percent about the people you lead and work with.

CARE PERSONALLY

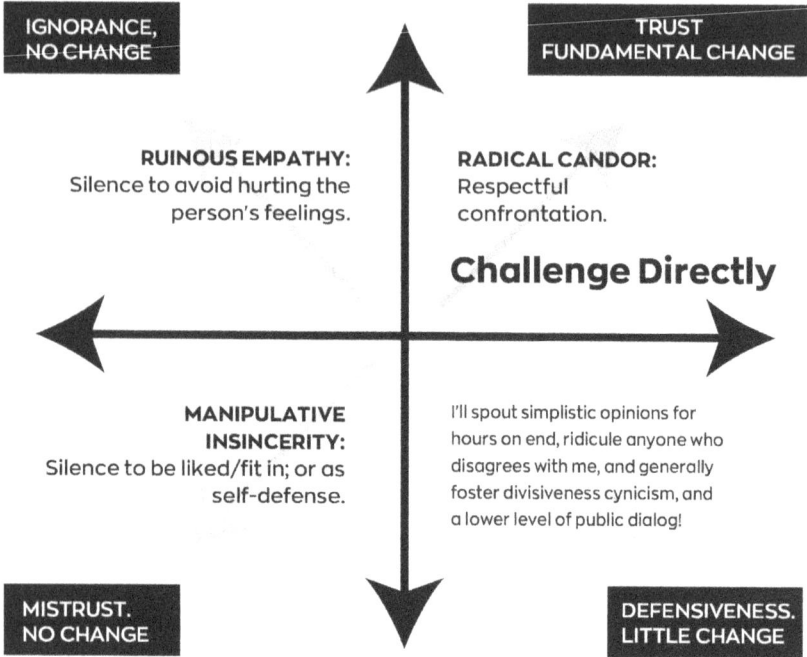

IGNORANCE,
NO CHANGE

TRUST
FUNDAMENTAL CHANGE

RUINOUS EMPATHY:
Silence to avoid hurting the
person's feelings.

RADICAL CANDOR:
Respectful
confrontation.

Challenge Directly

**MANIPULATIVE
INSINCERITY:**
Silence to be liked/fit in; or as
self-defense.

I'll spout simplistic opinions for
hours on end, ridicule anyone who
disagrees with me, and generally
foster divisiveness cynicism, and
a lower level of public dialog!

MISTRUST.
NO CHANGE

DEFENSIVENESS.
LITTLE CHANGE

Let's explore one more reason why loss and grief are so important. I briefly mentioned earlier in the book the notion of a three-day bereavement leave being unsustainable and totally inappropriate, especially during difficult times. So many of us, especially Western men, have been taught to "suck it up" when we experience a significant loss versus entering our deepest pain and processing it in a healthy way. And just as we've spoken about leadership, loss is very personal.

What can be a significant loss for one person may not be for another. I experienced this firsthand while coaching in the HPL program. I had an executive in my small coaching group who was deeply struggling when he arrived but had not been able to determine the exact reasons. He was seemingly lost in his day-to-day activities and had no passion for what he was doing. We discovered that he was in grief mode due to a promised promotion by his CEO that ultimately went to someone else. He was then able to process that grief and experience a true transformation in himself and his leadership. But other executives in the program said things to other coaches like, "That's just business." Or, "What's the big deal? He's still got a great job." One person's pain is another person's no-big-deal!

And that is what has happened globally with the Covid situation and other tumults since then. As with change and the 1-to-99 scale, it's important for all of us to recognize that not everyone is having the same perceptions of an experience. In the New Reality some of us have experienced substantial losses and others not so much. Some are exhilarated by working from home, and others are ready to stampede back to the office. We must embrace the fact that we are unique individuals, and one more time for emphasis: *One-size-fits-all leadership is officially dead!*

POINTS TO REMEMBER

- Leaders should care 100 percent about the people they lead.
- Becoming a secure base for those around you creates a deep level of psychological safety.

CHAPTER 21

LEADERSHIP AND MANAGEMENT STYLES

Management is doing things right.
Leadership is doing the right things.

—Peter Drucker

As we come to understand leadership at deeper levels through knowing who we are and understanding key insights for ourselves and others, let's apply these concepts to our leadership.

As I referenced in the Preface there are many ideas, concepts, and philosophies about management and leadership styles. One that many of us are familiar with is Abraham Maslow's hierarchy of needs that he proposed in 1943. He developed an ascending hierarchy, often represented as a pyramid, that shows our needs in two categories, deficiency needs and growth needs. The reason I'm mentioning Maslow first is that I believe his theory provides some validation for the ABL S.A.F.E.T.Y.™ model in that after our baseline physiological needs of air, water, food, and shelter are met, then safety needs come next. The third area is our need for belonging.[1]

Howard Ross, in his book *Our Search for Belonging*, challenges Maslow's theory and posits that belonging may actually be our baseline, or first need.[2] I do believe that the Covid situation and the New Reality has demonstrated that Ross may be correct, or if he's not, at least belonging should be placed in the same category of physiological needs like air and water. And it may also help explain some of the reasons for the Great Resignation. People are going to find places to work, even if they must start their own company, where they are valued first and foremost for who they are as a person and not what they produce. You could also argue that the baseline needs have been met by so many people that they are now pursuing the needs for love and belonging and seeking out places where they can fulfill those needs.

Another style of popular leadership is Situational Leadership. The original theory was developed in concert by Paul Hersey and Ken Blanchard and first introduced in 1969. The essence of the original Situational Leadership Theory, which was shortened to Situational Leadership by Hersey, is that we operate in four leadership behaviors: Telling (S1), Selling (S2), Participating (S3), and Delegating (S4). Those four behaviors are then utilized based on the audience's maturity level, which is also identified in four categories of maturity by the person or group being led: Unable and insecure (M1), Unable but confident (M2), Capable but unwilling (M3), and Very capable (M4).[3]

When Blanchard established his own company in 1977, he altered and advanced the model, relabeling it Situational Leadership II (SLII). The point is that leadership models and styles have been evolving over the decades.

The Blanchard Companies more recently performed a study that found 54 percent of us use and activate one style of leadership only.[4] Here's my question to you: If you're only using one style of leadership, how's that working for you?

Another model of leadership style that I believe has relevance for today's world is the model that Dan Goleman developed in his book *Primal Leadership*.[5] This book has fared well over time partly because it expands on a popular concept from his first book *Emotional Intelligence*.[6] The term emotional intelligence was created by two researchers, Peter Salavoy and John Mayer, in their article "Emotional Intelligence" in the journal *Imagination, Cognition, and Personality* in 1990.[7] But Dan Goleman is considered the father of EI, EQ, or emotional intelligence, due to the popularity of his books. EQ has become a foundational idea of what can separate good leadership from great leadership. I taught leadership in a master's and MBA program at two major universities, and I would tell the students that their IQ would get them hired, but their EQ would get them promoted. What exactly is EQ? It is recognizing, understanding, and managing our own emotions in the moment, which enables us to recognize, understand, and influence the emotions and outcomes of others.

Drawing from his work and writing on EQ in both books, Goleman and his team wrote a *Harvard Business Review* article titled "Leadership That Gets Results,"[8] where they provided research data on six different leadership styles and quantified their efficacy in positive or negative terms. That *HBR* article is said to be the most widely read *HBR* article in the publication's history.

This brings us to the powerful suggestion that rises out of situational leadership—using the best style for a given time that helps you drive the needed results. I won't go into the details since the resources are there for you to go much deeper on this topic, but understand these essentials: Do you really understand what your leadership style(s) are? Are they assisting you in being the best version of yourself as a leader? Are they the right styles for the moment? And are they the right styles for the people you are leading?

I have provided a chart of the six styles, and you will notice at the top of the header that Goleman and his team have quantified whether the styles are positive or negative.

THE SIX LEADERSHIP STYLES AT A GLANCE

	COERCIVE	VISIONARY	AFFILIATIVE	DEMOCRATIC	PACESETTING	COACHING
Overall impact on climate	**Negative**	**Most strongly positive**	**Positive**	**Positive**	**Negative**	**Positive**
The leader's modus operandi	Demands immediate compliance	Mobilizes people toward a vision	Creates harmony and builds emotional bonds	Forges consensus through participation	Sets high standards for performance	Develops people for the future
The style in a phrase	»» Do what I tell you ««	»» Come with me ««	»» People come first ««	»» What do you think ««	»» Do as I do, now ««	»» Try this ««
Underlying emotional intelligence competencies	Drive to achieve, initiative, self-control	Self-confidence, empathy, change catalyst	Empathy, building relationships, communication	Collaboration, team leadership, communication	Conscientious-ness, drive to achieve, initiative	Developing others, empathy, self-awareness
When the style works best	In a crisis, to kick start a turn-around, or with problem employees	When changes require a new vision, or when a clear direction is needed	To heal rifts in a team or to motivate people during stressful circumstances	To build buy-in or consensus, or to get input from valuable employees	To get quick results from a highly motivated and competent team	To help employee improve performance or develop long-term strengths

Understanding that leadership is in the eye of the beholder requires us to step back and recognize exactly what our default leadership styles are. Most of us operate with one or two different styles that may or may not work "for the moment." An example of a style that worked for the moment and then didn't come from an executive coaching project I did. The president of the division had been brought in four years prior to our engagement, and his task was to turn around a floundering, unprofitable business unit. He had succeeded in accomplishing the goal, and the division was prospering. But the employees weren't. Why? Because his default leadership style, which was necessary and effective for the turnaround venture, wasn't working anymore. He had moved fast and made drastic changes, including very tough decisions about certain products and people. And he continued in that mode. But now that the division was doing well, his pace-setting style was no longer appropriate and had created a division among his team of leaders. The VP of HR had recently quit because of his leadership style. It was now time for him to adopt a different style to sustain the success he had originally created. It took an intervention to affect the changes, and I'm happy to report that he was able to make a significant change in the way he led the division. And he kept his job!

One other leadership style that warrants mentioning, because it aligns with the UnCommon Leadership® model, is called Servant Leadership. This philosophy has been around for over 2,000 years in the teachings of Jesus, who said that he came to serve, not to be served, and provided the impetus for his disciples to do the same.

Fast forward to 1970, and Robert K. Greenleaf published an essay, "The Servant as Leader."[9] Greenleaf's definition is that the servant leader is first of all a servant, and "it begins with the natural feeling that one wants to serve." The Greenleaf Center for Servant Leadership further defines it as:

A philosophy and a set of practices that enriches the lives of individuals, builds better organizations, and ultimately creates a more just and caring world. This is a monumental shift from traditional leadership models where the focus is on strategy, goals, financial performance, and customer satisfaction to name just a few. The shift is on the employee and their growth and development— something that executives and leaders in today's marketplace should make as their number one priority.[10]

This servant leadership style has been adopted and expanded with great success, and I know a great person and company we could all emulate. I had the pleasure of spending time with Bob Chapman, the Chairman and CEO of Barry-Wehmiller, not long after his book was released. Bob has developed a leadership philosophy that, in my opinion, is very much aligned with, and based on, servant leadership. But he has taken it to another level and calls it Truly Human Leadership. His book *Everybody Matters*, co-written with Raj Sisodia,[11] is a phenomenal read and provides the details of what Truly Human Leadership looks like.

Chapman, like so many of us, took his college education and ran the company that his father had started, which he had taken over due to the untimely death of his father. He based his leadership style on KPI's,

MBO's, and any other management theory he had learned while earning his MBA at the University of Michigan. And at some level, he was successful as he had to turn around a company in financial distress. But Bob's leadership journey was altered due to events through which he realized that the people who worked for his company were someone's "precious child." That's the term that he came to use, and he realized that they should treat all their employees in that manner. He dramatically shifted his focus and the focus of his leadership team, and the results have been extraordinary. In the Great Recession of 2008, his philosophy was put to the test, and it passed with unbelievable results. What he and his leadership team have done is to create a company where every employee is valued.

They have created the psychological safety in their organization that we previously discussed, and they have the results to prove it works.

In fact, when Simon Sinek and Amy Cudy heard about Bob and Barry-Wehmiller, they were in disbelief that there was a company being run that way. They reached out to Bob, and he flew them to many of the company's locations so they could see first-hand the power of the company's culture and the effect it had on employees. My encouragement is to get his book and read further to discover another model that is probably the most closely aligned with the content of what you are now reading and with the UnCommon Leadership® model.

My meeting with Bob in his St. Louis office was a funny but serious event. We discussed leadership and our own philosophies for quite some time, and I explained about the HPL executive development program at IMD and the dramatic results it was producing for the leaders who attended. At one point I told him that we would tell the executives, "If you haven't figured out what this program is about, we're trying to bring humanity back to companies."

With that statement Bob slammed his hand down on the board room table and yelled, "Ed, you've read my book. We've never had humanity in our companies!"

He was indicating what we are faced with today—companies haven't focused on their people in a way that makes them feel valued, hence the Great Resignation.

Even after all the publicity due to Covid and talk about how to focus more on employees, I read a story about an employee who was reprimand-ed for being *26 seconds late* from her break. Seriously? Sadly, there may always be tone-deaf leaders. But if you've read this far in the book, you realize and hopefully embrace that we need a revolution. You and I can lead the way!

I'll wrap up this chapter with a final reminder. One style of leadership doesn't work. It has never worked, but after Covid and the New Reality, it's been exposed in ways that none of us could have previously imagined.

Let's move toward closing out this section and the book with informa-tion on how you can elevate your leadership in ways you may not realize are possible.

POINTS TO REMEMBER

- There are many models and styles of leadership. Most of us only use one.
- If you were to add another model or style of leadership, which one would expand your leadership capabilities the most?

CHAPTER 22

WHY DO WE MISS LEADING OTHERS? OUR INTRINSIC MOTIVATIONS ARE HIDDEN!

How we perceive ourselves and others
will motivate how we act and how we behave.
This means that our perceptions (and our misperceptions)
assume critical importance in how we live our lives.

—Dr. Roger Birkman

Leadership that makes a difference in your life and in the lives of people you're blessed to serve has another level most people never discover, or if they do, it's by trial and error and takes too much time. We've already discussed that what I want from my leader could be very different from what you want. We've looked at methods for finding that out, but there is an almost fool-proof method I discovered more than 20 years ago, and this chapter and the next will enlighten you!

After more than 70 years and many millions of people who have taken the Birkman Method® Assessment,[1] it is still one of the best-kept secrets in the assessment industry. When I mention that it is my assessment tool of choice, about 25 percent of the time people recognize and know about it.

Dr. Roger Birkman recognized and then developed an assessment to provide the deep insight that our perceptions are powerful drivers of how we see, judge, and value ourselves, others, and the world around us.

And notice the other word in his above quote—misperceptions. It is likely that many of the ideas we believe about others, about the world, and maybe ourselves, aren't accurate—just as I learned the hard way with my daughter. In the first section we discussed how the brain tries to make sense of the world around us and that it will, in fact, lie to us. Our perceptions, driven by our values, biases, interests, and passions, are the cognitive filters we use to judge experiences and people, and they are powerful drivers.

This presents the leadership challenge that when it comes to judging and perceiving people, what you see on the outside may not represent who that person is on the inside or what they need to become the best version of themselves. The intrinsic motivations of a person are, for the most part, hidden from our view. We see the outward persona (the person effect), and we assume that is the 360-degree view of the person.

And for many of us nothing could be further from the truth. What I've been able to quantify in more than three decades of using the Birkman Method assessment is that only ten percent of the population I've worked with are, for the most part, "what you see is what you get." Meaning that their intrinsic motivations, strengths, and possible stress reactions are mostly in the same category that the assessment measures. This indicates that we could potentially be missing with up to 90 percent of the people we're working with or leading and not understand why. Our misses could be very small, or they could be very big.

Dr. Birkman had a profound effect on me, as he did with most of us consultants who had the privilege of associating with him and his company, Birkman International, while he was alive. As I described earlier, this was a man who came to the office almost every day until he was 93 years old because of his mantra *"When you love what you do, it's not work!"*

His assessment is considered one of the most comprehensive, valid, and reliable assessments there is and to the best of my knowledge, the only one that provides the deep insight into a person's intrinsic motivations or needs.

I am fully aware that when the topic of assessments comes up, two very different reactions often come out. One is, "Tell me more. This sounds interesting and different." The other, more prevalent reaction, is, "Oh, no! Not another assessment." It seems that OD and HR people have been promoting and asking leadership teams to go through a myriad of different assessments with no real continuity or "stickiness" to help leaders apply the learning.

They will conduct a half-day or full-day workshop and then leave everyone to their own devices to implement the information they've obtained. Most of those efforts fail because they have no real plan for how to utilize the information from the assessment. Or there isn't even any information on how to use the assessment data to become a better leader. I can't tell you the number of times I've talked to leaders, and when I ask them what assessments they've used or been exposed to, their answer is something like, "We did this assessment one day that our HR team led [or an outside consultant brought in]. It was fun. We found out what four-letter, color or animal each of us was. I can't remember the name of the assessment, though, and we never did anything else with it after that."

This is a tragedy. It taints the mindset of people to have a negative view of assessments because they haven't seen the positive impact a good one can have on a person, a team, or an organization. This has been a disservice by well-intentioned people that has left a sour taste in the mouths of many leaders. If that description sounds familiar to you, please put aside the bias for a time and see if I can restore your faith that there is, in fact, an assessment that can elevate your leadership and those around you.

What Dr. Birkman, the creator of the Birkman Method® assessment, understood more than 70 years ago is that diversity of thought, freedom, empathy, change, and many other areas are key issues for the workplace. And he was way ahead of his time in developing an instrument that enabled us to truly understand the diversity of the people on the team and then use that information to harness the power of that diversity versus trying to lead and manage all of the people in the same manner.

In recent years we have seen a great intensity in the emergence of conversations regarding diversity, equity, and inclusion. It's a much-needed conversation, and the fact that companies are finally serious about this is welcome news after so many years of their saying they were committed to it but not being intentional about making it a priority.

When I do team workshops that deploy the Birkman Method® assessment, I usually lead with the idea that for most of us it's easy to get our heads around the idea of ethnic, religious, and racial diversity, but the area we may struggle with the most, both as leaders and followers, is diversity in how we operate, communicate, make decisions, lead, and want to be led.

I had an executive coaching assignment a few years ago in which the leader was told, "Shape up or ship out." In frustration one day he stated, "I know how to solve my problem. I'm going to hire people just like me!" I politely held the mirror back up and said, "No, that's why I'm here. You haven't figured out how to work with people who lead, manage, and follow differently from you."

In his case, it was the classic story of "if everyone in the room always agrees, then several of them probably aren't needed." And at that point he was the one who wasn't needed unless he was able to pivot and learn to value and embrace the differences of his team members.

Remember the Platinum Rule? *Do unto others as they would want to be done unto them.* Knowing what others want done unto them is the most effective way to successfully lead. Or another way to say it, the most effective way to successfully lead is to know what others need from their leader or their environment for their strengths to show up and be the very best version of themselves.

How do we do that? The Birkman Method® assessment is the perfect answer. My initial consultation and Birkman results came in 1999, and I elevated my use of the Birkman assessment in my leadership role after the feedback from my coach that I described in Chapter 18. The information I received gave me the exact data on how I needed to adjust my leadership style for some of my team members.

I could finally understand at a deeper level the true, intrinsic motivations of each team member. Going forward I began to use the Birkman in all of my leadership roles, my consulting engagements, and executive coaching assignments, and it had a profound impact on me, and my leadership, and gave me a tremendous ability to add instant value to my clients.

What makes the Birkman so different from most other assessments? As I previously mentioned, most assessments describe your usual style or behavior. Some manage to provide a bit more information, such as possible stressors or stress reactions. But the Birkman assessment not only reports what your usual style is—that is, what your strengths are—it also accurately *identifies your needs or intrinsic motivations* that must be addressed in your environment and relationships for the best version of you to show up. It then goes one step further and *identifies the potential stress behaviors* that may show up if the intrinsic motivations aren't met. This is *the best* social and emotional intelligence tool you can ever use.

I have mapped the Birkman data to the 18 competencies Dan Goleman outlined in his four-box EQ model: Self-Awareness, Self-Management, Social-Awareness, and Relationship Management. Of the 18 competencies, applying the Birkman data allows you to directly or indirectly ascertain how a person will approach 15 of the 18 competencies! I'm not aware of any other assessment that could provide that level of information and do it with a high degree of accuracy.

If you use assessments as a way of finding out how to lead people on a personal level, this information about the Birkman is important to understand, especially if you're not an HR or OD person who has had exposure to assessments throughout your career.

You will hear comments parroted a lot in the HR and OD fields about this or that assessment being 80 to 85 percent valid. What most are describing is *face validity*. 85-percent face validity is when I take the results from that assessment, consult the employee, and 85 percent of the time as we discuss the data, they say "Yes, that sounds like me." Then there is *test/retest reliability*, which is a different story. What that means is I can take the assessment today, take it again in a month, a year, or five years, and most of the data stays the same. Very few assessments have that level of reliability. The Birkman Method has some of the most reliable data, even though it measures over 60 dimensions of a person.

Since many others have written articles indicating the challenges with the Meyers-Briggs Type Indicator assessment (MBTI), I'll go a step further with the comparison as it is probably the most ubiquitous assessment on the market. Many people claim it is 80 to 90 percent valid. Yes, when you hear that you are an INFJ you go, "Yep, that's me!"

But here is what can and will happen. Before discovering the Birkman Method, I used the MBTI in my leadership roles. I have taken that assessment many times at different points in my life. I have results that show I am an ENFP, ENFJ, INFP, and INFJ! So, which is it? That's the point I suggest that you consider—are you getting accurate information about yourself and the people that you're leading? If the assessment is not reliable and valid, then move on. How do you know if it's reliable? Ask for the technical manual and how they measure the dimensions that are measured, and you'll have your answer.

I have placed the Birkman technical manual in the hands of two IO psychologists, and both were stunned by the level of validity and reliability. I won't go into the methodology used because that is also part of the reliability that is created—not knowing the construct of the assessment before taking it. Dr. Birkman figured out something a long time ago about our truly unique perceptions and developed an assessment that is head and shoulders above most others.

I hope you can now begin to understand just how powerful the Birkman Method can be. I am devoting a lot of space in this book to the Birkman, and I do so because I've seen and lived out how different and useful it can be to help you become a better leader to help those you work with or lead. Because the assessment measures over 60 dimensions of a person, I won't go into the details, but I will explain some of the more useful examples of how this assessment can be used to grow and strengthen you as a person and a leader.

Let's look first at the concept of change as I discussed earlier in Chapter 7. There are many beliefs in the public domain about change and how people approach change and we discussed previously two primary opinions: that people resist change itself, and that people resist the pain of change. The truth is that both of those could be right, but change is personal, and each of us has a profile regarding change that can be very different from each other, so putting people into two boxes does a disservice to anyone along a wide spectrum of those two ideas.

The Birkman Method assessment reports nine (9) key components that provide a holistic view of ourselves and there are two components that allow us to predict with a high degree of accuracy exactly how each of us will approach change. The components are called Restlessness and Insistence. Restlessness provides information on how a person focuses their attention or prefers to seek variety in their day-to-day activities. The Insistence component provides information on a person's approach to detail, structure, follow-through, and daily routines.

The assessment provides three key pieces of data that are represented on a 1-to-99 intensity scale. I can see exactly what the person's usual style or strengths are, which means whether they want variety, or they want to focus on what is in front of them, or are possibly somewhere in the middle. And we are also provided the potential stress behaviors that may arise if a person's needs (or intrinsic motivations) aren't met by the environment or the people that a person is working with.

For example, a high Restlessness usual style score predicts that a person is responsive to external stimuli, will embrace change in terms of daily variety, likes different tasks throughout their day, and finds it easy to rapidly shift focus. When it comes to day-to-day change, the low-Restlessness-score individual prefers limited changes as they prefer to remain focused, are comfortable staying on the same task for long periods of time, and want to be free of external interruptions and outwardly imposed change while they are on task.

When it comes to the concept of overall organizational change, the Insistence component provides even more information about how someone would approach change. The high-Insistence person probably struggles with too much change if it is perceived as too fast or disruptive. They prefer consistency, and precedent matters. The lower-Insistence-score person will tend to be less attached to "the ways we've always done it," and because they find it easier to embrace the "new" and can be spontaneous and flexible, they may also appear to go with the flow and more readily accept big and sweeping organizational changes.

From more than 70 years of tracking the data, we know that most people cluster around the middle of the 1-to-99 spectrum on the Restlessness component, so that predicts that most people require a balance of consistency and normalcy and some variety and change of focus in their day-to-day activities. However, the Insistence scoring pattern does provide a clue that "most" people are on the higher end of the scoring pattern and therefore possibly more resistant to organizational changes. When someone is outside of these normative scores and we have that information it can provide great insight as a leader into how to approach our teams on a day-to-day basis, especially if there are going to be significant changes to our group, department, division, or company. We will know with a high degree of accuracy who can easily be our champions and who we need to focus on to gain their buy-in for the changes that we are making.

As I referenced earlier, but it's important to amplify, if all that we had were the usual style or strengths descriptions, that would be good information, but *what makes the Birkman assessment so powerful—in addition to its unparalleled consistency and accuracy—is that it also provides the Platinum Rule data.* This is the magic and power of the Birkman. It tells us what each of us *needs* in order to access our strengths, and for many of us, me included, that can be very different from our usual style.

The final piece of data the Birkman provides us, as I mentioned, is that it also tells us the indications of the potential stress behaviors should a person's needs go unmet in a particular area. With this information, I no longer need to guess how each of my team members approach change, need change, or will resist change versus a one-size-fits-all approach.

From Birkman International, here are the areas that the assessment covers:

- Usual Behavior—effective behavioral styles for tasks and relationships
- Underlying Needs—internal perceptions and expectations for how tasks and relationships should be governed
- Stress Behavior—ineffective behavioral styles when needs go unmet
- Interests—vocational and avocational preferences
- Occupational—22 job families, 200+ job titles (linked to O*Net)
- Management Styles—approach to managing tasks and people[2]

As you can see, the assessment is exceptionally comprehensive, and this data is provided with one unified set of questions versus some other assessments that require you to take two, three, or even four different questionnaires.

I hope that what you've read so far has piqued your curiosity in that there is an assessment that could help transform your leadership for both yourself and others. When I received my consultation in 1999, light bulbs went on for me in that I knew there was an underlying tension between who I was on the outside versus who I was on the inside and what my needs were.

Today, armed with accurate data about who I am, my standard joke when I do a consultation and use myself as an example to help others understand their own personal reports is that once I saw my Birkman reports, it explained the fact that I not only might confuse you with my leadership style, but I just might confuse myself! How is this possible? Because who I am on the outside is a very busy, action-focused, results-oriented leader. *But* to be the *best* version of myself I need downtime and rest time.

The fact that I could lay on a couch and read a book for a weekend would surprise a lot of people who only know my get-it-done, make-it-happen outward persona.

Out of the many Birkman consultations I've done both one-to-one and one-to-many, let me tell a few stories to more fully express how powerful this information can be for us as leaders and followers, and how it gives us the roadmap, or user's manual, for implementing this idea that leadership is personal, and personalized, and that it is in the eye of the follower.

When I was president, I had a CTO for my division. He was an amazing person and was very personable. He was great to work with and typically was very congenial in our team meetings and worked to get along with the other members of our leadership team.

But one day in a series of morning meetings I saw a side of Fred that I hadn't previously seen. He was abrupt and even rude to some people. Short and curt with some of his answers, it was a very different person than I typically saw day in and day out.

When we finished the last meeting that morning, I went back to my office and pulled out Fred's Birkman reports. After a few minutes of reading, I realized what was going on. I called and asked him if he could clear his calendar and have lunch with me. He said yes and soon we were off to lunch. We ate and talked for a good 90 minutes, and toward the end Fred slumped down in his chair and said, "Thanks for inviting me to lunch and hearing me out today. I really needed that."

My response was, "Fred, I know you needed this lunch meeting. I'm very sorry. I saw some behaviors exhibited by you this morning that weren't usually present. I saw a man in stress mode, so I read your Birkman reports after our last meeting and realized that I was the cause of your stress. I have canceled our last three one-to-one meetings, and we haven't had one for more than two months. What your Birkman information reminded me of is how important it is for you to be valued and heard by your leader, and in that regard I've failed you. Here's my promise: I won't cancel and not reschedule our one-to-one meetings going forward because I realize how important they are to you. You are a key member of our team, and I need to value you in that manner going forward. Please accept my apologies."

Here's another quick story that also provides insight into the amount of information you would receive about yourself or others on your team from the Birkman. A few years ago, I was providing a consultation to a 25-year-old graduate student at USC who was a graduate assistant for the great leadership expert Warren Bennis. We were going through his data, and while doing so I was describing the UnCommon Leadership® model of personal and personalized leadership and how this information would assist a person to understand themselves and others at deeper and more accurate levels. He was captivated by the conversation and the information but at one point responded, "This leadership stuff sounds exhausting!" Maybe as you've read this book you've had a similar reaction. Yes, becoming an UnCommon Leader requires effort, intentionality, and focus, but it's worth it.

I have also performed consultations for several married couples and have seen how powerful the information is to bridge the gaps between them. One day I did a joint consultation with a couple. At one point I described to Sue that in stress mode she should realize that her stress behavior might take her further from getting her needs met when it came to how busy and active she was. Unknowingly, I uttered a phrase that set her off. "Sue, when you are in stress mode, consider that you might want to find something that you enjoy doing and get busy! Don't go take a nap or rest as that is not what your intrinsic needs are as indicated by the Birkman data."

With that statement, she slammed her hand down on the table, jumped up, and began screaming at her husband, "Are you listening to him, Mark? I've been trying to tell you for 25 years that I don't want to take a nap, and you won't listen!" I wish I had a picture of Mark as this was happening. It was priceless! She began circling the table we were sitting at and kept yelling at Mark for quite some time. The scene was intense on one hand, but it finally became funny for all of us to reflect on her reaction. It became a poignant and transformative moment for their relationship.

Why was this such a huge breakthrough for them? What had Mark been doing for 25 years? He was practicing the Golden Rule because in stress mode he needed to take a nap and thought that if that is what he needed, so did his wife. But she needed the Platinum Rule—for him to understand that being busy and active was her antidote for stress, not taking a nap.

One last story. During a consultation on Birkman data with a woman I'll call Linda, she began to cry. Why? Because the information was describing her in positive terms. All her life she had negative labels (beliefs) imprinted in her mind about who she was. She had always seen herself in good or bad terms, mostly bad. The information gave her a new way to think about herself that she hadn't thought of before. That's a lot of power in the hands of a consultant. I take that power very seriously and make it a point to highlight people's strengths when doing a consultation.

From my personal association with Dr. Birkman, I know what his intent was, and I am inspired and humbled to be able to stand on his shoulders to continue that intent. He wanted you to understand who you are and what you need to be the best version of yourself, to manage your stress better, and to see how strong, powerful and beautiful you are. He wanted you to feel positive after the consultation. And to experience that as a consultant and coach gives a feeling that I don't have words to describe.

If you are a leader, here are two questions to consider. Do you know what the people that you are working with need from you and expect from you? And have you figured out that how you lead Joe does not work for how you lead Mary? If so, I believe that you're ahead of the game as a leader. But in the executive coaching and team programs I've been doing and leading for decades, this is a huge area of growth for most leaders, just as it originally was for me.

POINTS TO REMEMBER

- Our perceptions are powerful—and they can be wrong.
- How you see people perform on the outside may not be who they are on the inside.

CHAPTER 23

HARNESSING THE POWER OF THE TEAM

Teamwork is the ability to work together toward a common vision.
The ability to direct individual accomplishments
toward organizational objectives.
It is the fuel that allows common people to achieve uncommon results.

—Andrew Carnegie

I have performed countless team programs around the world, and I would be remiss if I didn't cover, even briefly, how powerful the Birkman Method is for harnessing the power of teams and creating high-performing teams.

If it's only you and no one else, the Birkman Method assessment can help you understand yourself better, just as it did for me. But once you add one more person to the equation, relational dynamics come into play, and it is new math. One plus one doesn't equal two. It could equal three or five or even ten if the differences between the two people are abundant. And once you add a third person to the team, then all bets are off as to how they will work together. The exponential factor of how we get along when we have three or more people can't be quantified if you remember that the Birkman measures over 60 dimensions of a person. We are complicated people! Most of us have heard about the team methodology of "forming, storming, norming, and performing," and without a Birkman assessment to help understand the dynamics of all of the team members, you may stay in the storming phase too long.

Here's a story to amplify how powerful the Birkman can be for teams. I was conducting a two-day workshop for a CIO, whom I'll call Kristine, and her team of 22 people. On the second day we were doing a deep dive into their individual Birkman data, and the CIO permitted me to ask this question: "Is there something about her leadership style that you wish she would change or do differently?"

One of her key VPs jumped at the chance to answer in the safe environment we had produced and said, "When we're in meetings, Kristine makes very fast decisions about what she wants to happen. The rest of us are immediately thinking about the who, what, where, when, and how we're going to implement the decision that was just made. But Kristine is ready to move on to the next topic or idea and doesn't give us a chance to discuss, debate, and get our heads around the decision she's just made. It's very frustrating for us."

I wish you could have seen the look on the CIO's face! She was stunned for the moment, but she leaned in, and we had a very robust conversation on how the team could create dialogue, such that when she was exercising her strength of making quick decisions and moving on, the team could alert her that they needed time to work it out.

I asked the VP what had kept her from telling this to the CIO, and her response was classic. "She's the CIO. We must adjust to her leadership, but it's been very frustrating!" How many of us as C-suite leaders provide an atmosphere where our team has permission to challenge or call out the leader in the moment? Very few. This is the essence of *leadership is in the eye of the beholder!* What the Birkman assessment can help us do is reduce the time and possibly eliminate the storming part of the equation.

I've indicated how one result of my consultations is that people occasionally cry. To show you that this isn't exclusively a gender thing, here's one last story. A few years ago, I was doing a one-day team program for seven male leaders. One of the ways we help the team members understand themselves and how they work or don't work together is what I call a *line-up* exercise. We take the Components of the assessment data and turn an area of the room into a 1-to-99 spectrum. We then walk through the three dimensions of some of the components, especially those that impact relationships. On this day we had gone through three of the components, and each time one person, whom I'll call Rick, seemed very different from the rest of the team. At one point he began to cry. I still have flashbacks of how powerful that moment was. We had created a psychologically safe environment that allowed him to be his authentic self. As we all paused to allow Rick to breathe and talk about his tears, his words made some of us cry too. He told us he had always felt different, and because of that life had been a struggle. His tears were not sad tears; they were breakthrough tears. He now felt understood at a level he had never before experienced.

I think that by now you have the picture of why I am such an evangelist for the Birkman Method® assessment. I have seen relationships repaired and restored. I have experienced people realizing for the first time in their life that there was power in who they were versus the negative label they or others had put on them. I have seen teams begin to perform at new levels of productivity and inclusion. I could probably write as many words as are contained in this book in telling the many stories I've experienced.

POINTS TO REMEMBER

- One plus one doesn't equal two when it comes to relational dynamics
- Team dynamics present a completely different challenge for leaders.
- The Birkman Method® assessment can shorten the time needed for the team to arrive at the performing stage.

LEADERSHIP IS IN THE EYE OF THE BEHOLDER

The workplace of today and tomorrow will be affected by the events of the Covid situation for quite some time if not forever. It is imperative that leaders embrace the teachings of this section to recognize that leadership is truly personal and personalized. Who am I as a leader? How do I affect people with my leadership? What do THEY want and expect from their leader(s)? Do I really understand the intrinsic motivations of the people that I lead? Do I understand what true psychological safety means and that it is personal as well?

This section has provided a deep dive into the many facets of what it looks like to get very intentional about discovering who you are as a leader and how you lead others. We can no longer take the usual path of just doing what we do without any recognition of its impact. The people have spoken with their feet and their willingness to tolerate poor leadership is over.

I provided a reference in this section to Howard Ross's work in his book *Our Search for Belonging* and I will guide you toward an article that you can find in the reference section of this book from the Future Forum and their launch of the Remote Employee Experience Index quarterly survey. The Future Forum is a consortium of companies led by Slack and the initial data is the result of surveying 4,700 employees. The survey found these key facts:

- People prefer choice in their working environment—72 percent want a mix of in-office and remote work.
- Remote work is a net positive—knowledge workers report higher levels of satisfaction with remote work compared to office work.
- **But not for everyone!** *Worker's sense of belonging can suffer while working remotely.* Experienced employees had a higher level of satisfaction and productivity than their less experienced peers.
- Relationships matter—*connection is the biggest challenge to remote work.*[1]

The Future Forum has continued to provide ongoing research and as recently as January, 2022, the number of employees surveyed that want location flexibility is 78 percent along with 68 percent still wanting hybrid work arrangements. These two pieces of data have radically shifted the employment market as well as what workers want.[2]

You can see in The Future Forum's research the quantification of how important "belonging" is to us humans! To repeat one more time for emphasis, never has it been more obvious that leadership is personal and personalized, and a significant part of this equation is creating a psychologically safe environment where people feel wanted, accepted, and "belonged!" There—I've just created a new adjective to describe the essence of this section. We must extend our efforts in developing ourselves, becoming more aware of who we are—I want to belong, you want to belong, and so does everyone else!

FINAL THOUGHT

Maybe after reading this book, you have the same reaction as the young man in the story from a previous chapter who felt that this leadership thing could be exhausting. But apart from exhaustion or complication, the primary requirements are to become aware and intentional.

My hope is that you've been inspired to do the work to be the best leader for yourself and for those that you lead now or in the future. This also means to be the best version of yourself and to help others be the same. When we have the resources to drive toward a new level of leadership for ourselves and others, leadership doesn't have to be exhausting. On the contrary, UnCommon Leadership® is exhilarating.

One-size-fits-all leadership is dead. May it Rest in Peace.

ARE YOU READY TO BECOME AN UNCOMMON LEADER?

E d Chaffin would love to help you make that happen. The insights shared throughout this book are the foundational principles that he uses when coaching, training and inspiring leaders around the world to elevate performance and achieve their highest potential.

Lift these principles off of the page and invite them into your life or the lives of the leaders within your company by inviting Ed to speak to your team or organization or engage him in executive coaching or team workshops.

Speaking

Discover the source that keeps leaders from reaching their full potential. With decades of immersive experience leading teams and organizations to success, Ed inspires leaders to create an impact by transforming themselves in the process through his memorable keynotes, workshops and training.

Assessment

The Birkman Method® Assessment is a meaningful tool to facilitate personal growth, and Ed leverages this proven method to reveal each person's unique personality and identify how it impacts their individual leadership approach. Request an individual or team assessment and unlock the knowledge you need for meaningful growth.

Coaching

From executive coaching to team transformation workshops, Ed helps leaders leverage their strengths and intrinsic motivations to become the best versions of themselves and inspire their teams to achieve better results. Reach out to learn how Ed can support you and your team.

To learn how you can bring his message to you or your organization, visit www.edchaffin.com or reach out via email at ed@edchaffin.com.

REVIEW INQUIRY

Hey, it's Ed here. As you've learned from the book, readers are never not leading. (And they are always sharing!)

I wrote *UnCommon Leadership® for the New Reality* as a resource for individuals wanting to become their best selves, make a difference in the lives of others, and create a meaningful legacy through their leadership efforts.

Would you write a review?

If you enjoyed the book and are finding it useful in your life, consider giving Ed a simple, but extremely impactful, thank you by writing a review. Rating the book and writing a meaningful review will not only let me know that this book has impacted your life, but it will also help other leaders know that the book is worth reading as well.

Would you consider providing a meaningful review on Amazon, Goodreads, or another online store where you purchased the book or are actively a part of? Online bookstores are more likely to spread the word about a book when they know that the book is making an impact. And, reviews help. Your review could help more leaders become UnCommon Leaders, and let's be honest, our world could use as many UnCommon Leaders as it can get.

WILL YOU SHARE THE LOVE?

Would you share this book with others who may benefit from it?

Some gifts you outgrow. Others will break. But the best will not just change the life of the gift receiver, but of everyone they meet. The gift of UnCommon Leadership could very well do just that.

If you loved this book, consider gifting it to others in your life who could benefit from the principles shared. Get a copy to give to a friend, an associate, an aspiring leader, or a family member. I've come to find that leaders never stop leading, but UnCommon Leaders know the value in sharing what they have learned with others, too.

Special bulk discounts are available if you would like to give a copy to your entire team or organization. Visit www.edchaffin.com to learn more, or contact me directly at ed@edchaffin.com.

Many thanks in advance,
Ed Chaffin

ENDNOTES

Preface

1. Bersin, Josh. "The Year of the Employee: Predictions For Talent, Leadership, And HR Technology In 2014." *Forbes*, December 19, 2013.

2. Glaser, Edward and Cutler, David. "You may get more work done at home. But you'd have better ideas at the office." *The Washington Post*, September 24, 2021. https://www.washingtonpost.com/outlook/2021/09/24/working-home-productivity-pandemic-remote/.
   Maurer, Roy. "Study Finds Productivity Not Deterred by Shift to Remote Work." Society for Human Resource Management, September 16, 2020. https://www.shrm.org/hr-today/news/hr-news/Pages/Study-Productivity-Shift-Remote-Work-COVID-Coronavirus.aspx.

3. Axon, Samuel. "Apple has a new work-from-home policy, but it's still not what employees want." *Arstechnica*, November 19, 2021. https://arstechnica.com/gadgets/2021/11/apple-employees-will-return-to-the-office-this-february-leaked-cook-email-says/.

4. Cohen, Arianne. "Chaos Control." *Korn Ferry Briefings*, February and March, 2022. https://www.kornferry.com/insights/briefings-magazine/issue-53/

chaos-control?utm_source=marketo&utm_medium=email&utm_term=&utm_content=briefings&utm_campaign=15-02-gbl-briefings-issue-53&mkt_tok=NDk0LVZVQ5y00ODIAAAGCnLRzyAZJ8dwcNwkztAaSIYn993Q7EgS-VCN-dKxUyZhRw1ko8rDZOEMRWswwCpY5Wu0Brzx8fLekcZvl5KDhuNfkM7fBJFdjNrp5IMQqqnO-zOo).

Introduction

1. Wiles, Jackie. "Employees Seek Personal Value and Purpose at Work." Gartner, January 13, 2022. https://www.gartner.com/en/articles/employees-seek-personal-value-and-purpose-at-work-be-prepared-to-deliver.
2. Jolton, Jeffrey, Ph.D and Hayes, Bryan, Ph.D. "Big Data Helps Bust Three Myths of Employee Engagement and Leadership." IBM Smarter Workforce Institute, February, 2014. https://content.lesaffaires.com/LAF/lacom/IBM_3_myths.PDF.

Chapter 1

1. Lipton, Bruce. *The Biology of Belief: Unleashing the Power of Consciousness, Matter, and Miracles.* Carlsbad, CA: Hay House Inc., 2005.
2. Church, Dawson. *Mind to Matter: The Astonishing Science of How Your Brain Creates Material Reality.* Carlsbad, CA: Hay House, 2018.
3. Dispenza, Joe. "How I Healed Myself After Breaking 6 Vertebrae." Healyourlife.com, May 23, 2014. https://www.healyourlife.com/how-i-healed-myself-after-breaking-6-vertebrae.
4. Barker, Clifton. "Embracing Stress Is More Important than Reducing Stress." *Stanford News*, May 7, 2015. https://news.stanford.edu/2015/05/07/stress-embrace-mcgonigal-050715/.

Chapter 2

1. Rowbotham, Samuel. *Earth Not a Globe,* London, 1881.
2. Josa, Clare. *Ditching Imposter Syndrome.* n.p.: Beyond Alchemy Publishing, 2020.
3. Clance, Pauline R. and Imes, Suzanne A. "The Impostor Phenomenon in High Achieving Women: Dynamics and Therapeutic Intervention." *Psychotherapy: Theory, Research & Practice,* 15(3), 241–247, 1978.

Chapter 3

1. Goldsmith, Marshall. *Triggers: Creating Behavior That Lasts—Becoming the Person You Want to Be.* New York: Crown Publishing Group, 2015.
2. Thomas, Julia. "What Is the Preconscious and What Does It Mean to Me?" *Better Help*, February 1, 2021. https://www.betterhelp.com/advice/general/what-is-the-preconscious-and-what-does-it-mean-to-me/.
3. Peer, Marisa. "To reach beyond your limits by training your mind," TEDxKCS, January 22, 2015. https://www.youtube.com/watch?v=zCv-ZBy6_yU.
4. Edberg, Henrik. "Arnold Schwarzenegger's Top 5 Tips for Building the Life You Want." The Positivity Blog, April 15, 2021. https://www.positivityblog.com/arnold-schwarzeneggers-top-5-tips-for-building-the-life-you-want/.
5. Dispenza, Joe. "How I Healed Myself After Breaking 6 Vertebrae." Healyourlife.com, May 23, 2014. https://www.healyourlife.com/how-i-healed-myself-after-breaking-6-vertebrae.

Chapter 4

1. Nightingale, Earl. *The Strangest Secret*. Nightingale-McHugh Company, 1956.
2. Alcock, James E., Ph.D. "We Are Our Beliefs." *Psychology Today*, February 14, 2018. https://www.psychologytoday.com/us/blog/belief/201802/we-are-our-beliefs

Chapter 5

1. Warmerdam, Gary van. *Mindworks: A Practical Guide for Changing Thoughts, Beliefs, and Emotional Reactions*. Santa Barbara, CA: Cairn Publishing, 2014.
2. Warmerdam, Gary van. "How to Change Beliefs." YouTube, November 17, 2017. https://www.youtube.com/watch?v=PxditxbHsWg.
3. Mandino, Og. *The Greatest Salesman in the World*. Hollywood, FL: Frederick Fell Publishers, Inc., 1968, 2001, p. 44.
4. Maltz, Maxwell. Psycho-Cybernetics. New York, NY: Simon & Schuster, 1960.
5. RR, Wing, RW, Jeffrey. "Benefits of recruiting participants with friends and increasing social support for weight loss and maintenance." *Journal of Consulting and Clinical Psychology.* February, 1999. https://pubmed.ncbi.nlm.nih.gov/10028217/
6. Dweck, Carol. *Mindset: The New Psychology of Success*. New York, NY: Ballantine Books, 2007.

Chapter 6

1. Spiegel, Alex. "Teachers' Expectations Can Influence How Students Perform." NPR, September 17, 2012.

https://www.npr.org/sections/health-shots/2012/09/18/161159263/teachers-expectations-can-influence-how-students-perform.

2. Manzoni, Jean Francois and Barsoux, Jean-Louis. *The Set-Up-To-Fail Syndrome: How Good Managers Cause Great People to Fail.* Boston, MA: Harvard Business Review Press, 2002.

Chapter 7

1. *America's Got Talent*, YouTube, May 29, 2018. https://www.youtube.com/watch?v=8e0z3-iZ_TY.

2. Dweck, Carol. *Mindset: The New Psychology of Success.* New York, NY: Ballantine Books, 2007.

3. Ericcson, K. Anders, Prietula, Michael J., and Cokely, Edward T. "The Making of an Expert." *Harvard Business Review*, July–August 2007. https://hbr.org/2007/07/the-making-of-an-expert.

4. Gladwell, Malcolm. *Outliers: The Story of Success.* Boston, MA: Little, Brown and Company, 2008.

Chapter 8

1. Geronimi, Clyde et al. *Alice in Wonderland.* Walt Disney Productions, 1951.

2. Kotter, John. "Leading Change: Why Transformation Efforts Fail." *Harvard Business Review*. January, 2007. https://hbr.org/2007/01/leading-change-why-transformation-efforts-fail.

3. Posner, Barry and Kouzes, Jim. *The Leadership Challenge: How to Make Extraordinary Things Happen in Organizations,* sixth edition. San Francisco, CA: Jossey-Bass, 2017.

4. Wiles, Jackie. "Employees Seek Personal Value and Purpose at Work." Gartner, January 13, 2022. https://www.gartner.com/en/articles/

employees-seek-personal-value-and-purpose-at-work-be-prepared-to-deliver.

5. United States Department of Labor. March 29, 22. https://www.bls.gov/news.release/jolts.t04.htm#jolts_table4.f.p

6. De Smet, Aaron. Dowling, Bonnie, Mugayar-Baldocchi, Marino, and Schaninger, Bill. "'Great Attrition' or 'Great Attraction'? The choice is yours." *McKinsey Quarterly.* September 8, 2021. https://www.mckinsey.com/business-functions/people-and-organizational-performance/our-insights/great-attrition-or-great-attraction-the-choice-is-yours

7. Jolton, Jeffrey, Ph.D and Hayes, Bryan, Ph.D. "Big Data Helps Bust Three Myths of Employee Engagement and Leadership." IBM Smarter Workforce Institute, February, 2014. https://content.lesaffaires.com/LAF/lacom/IBM_3_myths.PDF.

8. Sutton, Robert. *The No Asshole Rule: Building a Civilized Workplace and Surviving One That Isn't.* New York, NY: Business Plus, Hachette Book Group, 2007.

9. Castrillon, Caroline. "Why Your Bad Boss Could Be Killing You." *Forbes.* July 21, 2019. https://www.forbes.com/sites/carolinecastrillon/2019/07/21/why-your-bad-boss-could-literally-be-killing-you/.

10. Nyberg, A. et al. "Managerial leadership and ischaemic heart disease among employees: the Swedish WOLF study." Journal of Occupational and Environmental Medicine. January, 2009. https://www.ncbi.nlm.nih.gov/pmc/articles/PMC2602855/

Chapter 10

1. Selig, Meg. "9 Surprising Superpowers of Knowing Your Core Values." *Psychology Today.* November 27, 2018. https://www.psychologytoday.com/us/blog/changepower/201811/9-surprising-superpowers-knowing-your-core-values

Chapter 11

1. Covey, Stephen. *The 7 Habits of Highly Successful People.* New York, NY: Simon & Schuster, 1989, 2004, 2013, 2020.

Chapter 12

1. George,Bill. *Discover Your True North.* Hoboken, NJ: John Wiley & Sons, Inc., 2015.
2. Kennedy, John F. "We Choose to Go to the Moon." Speech. Rice University, September 12, 1962.
3. Posner, Barry and Kouzes, Jim. "Inspire a Shared Vision." The Leadership Challenge, n.d., https://www.leadershipchallenge.com/ Research/Five-Practices.aspx.
4. Sinek, Simon. "How Great Leaders Inspire Action." TED Talk, March 10, 2014. https://www.ted.com/talks/ simon_sinek_how_great_leaders_inspire_action?language=en.

Chapter 14

1. Rath, Tom and Conchie, Barry. "What Followers Want From Leaders." Gallup. January 8, 2009. https://news.gallup.com/ businessjournal/113542/what-followers-want-from-leaders.aspx.

Wrap-Up For Principle #2

1. https://www.cbsnews.com/news/ ceo-pay-300-worker-salaries-compensation/

Chapter 16

1. Vatansever, Deniz, Menon, David K., and Stamatakis, Emmanuel A. "Default mode contributions to automated information processing." PNAS, October 23, 2017. https://www.pnas.org/doi/full/10.1073/pnas.1710521114

Chapter 17

1. Church, Dawson. *Mind to Matter: The Astonishing Science of How Your Brain Creates Material Reality.* Carlsbad, CA: Hay House, 2018.
2. Rogers, Bruce. "Our Brains Need Breaks From Virtual Meetings." *Forbes.* March 20, 2021. https://www.forbes.com/sites/brucerogers/2021/04/20/our-brains-need-breaks-from-virtual-meetings/?sh=154e230221e9

Chapter 19

1. "Guide: Understand team effectiveness." re:Work. n.d. https://rework.withgoogle.com/print/guides/5721312655835136/
2. *The Flintstones.* Hanna-Barbera Productions. 1960–1966.
3. The Academy of Brain-based Leadership. https://brainleadership.com.
4. Stewart, Henry. "8 companies that celebrate mistakes." Happy.co.uk. June 8, 2015. https://www.happy.co.uk/blogs/8-companies-that-celebrate-mistakes/
5. D. Radecki, L. Hull, J. McCusker and C. Ancona. *Psychological Safety: The key to happy, high performing people and teams.* Red Hill Publishing, 2018.

Chapter 20

1. Ainsworth, MD, Wittig, BA, Foss, BM. "The development of infant-mother interaction among the Ganda." *Determinants of infant behavior.* New York: Wiley; 1963. pp. 67–112.
2. Bowlby, J. *Attachment and loss: Vol. 1. Attachment.* 2. New York: Basic Books; 1969/1982.
3. Kohlrieser, George. *Hostage At The Table: How Leaders Can Overcome Conflict, Influence Others and Raise Performance.* San Francisco, CA: Jossey-Bass, 2006.
4. Kohlrieser, George, Goldsworthy, Susan, and Coombe, Duncan. *Care To Dare: Unleashing Astonishing Potential Through Secure Base.* San Francisco, CA: Jossey-Bass, 2012.
5. Scott,Kim. *Radical Candor: How to Get What You Want by Saying What You Mean.* New York: St. Martin's Press, 2017; London: Pan MacMillan, 2019.

Chapter 21

1. McLeod, Saul. "Maslow's Hierarchy of Needs." *Simply Psychology.* December 29, 2020. https://www.simplypsychology.org/maslow.html
2. Ross, Howard. *Our Search for Belonging: How Our Need to Connect Is Tearing Us Apart.* Oakland, CA: Berrett-Koehler Publishers, 2018.
3. Hersey, Paul and Blanchard, Ken. *The Situational Leader.* Morrisville, North Carolina: Center for Leadership Studies, 1984.
4. "Getting to Know the LBAII." The Ken Blanchard Companies. n.d. https://www.kenblanchard.com/Solutions/SLII
5. Goleman, Dan, Boyatzis, Richard, and McKee, Annie. *Primal Leadership: Unleashing the Power of Emotional Intelligence.* Boston: Harvard Business Review Press, 1999, 2013.
6. Goleman, Dan. *Emotional Intelligence: Why It Can Matter More than IQ.* New York: Random House, 1995; London: Bloomsbury Publishing, 1996, 2020.

7. Salavoy, Peter and Mayer, John. "Emotional Intelligence." *Imagination, Cognition, and Personality*, 9, 185–211, 1990. https://scholars.unh.edu/psych_facpub/450/

8. Goleman, Dan. "Leadership That Gets Results." *Harvard Business Review*. March–April, 2000. https://hbr.org/2000/03/leadership-that-gets-results.

9. Greenleaf, Robert. "The Servant as Leader." South Orange, NJ: Robert E. Greenleaf Center for Servant Leadership, 1970.

10. "What is Servant Leadership?" Robert E. Greenleaf Center for Servant Leadership, n.d., https://www.greenleaf.org/what-is-servant-leadership/.

11. Chapman, Bob and Sisodia, Raj. *Everybody Matters: The Extraordinary Power of Caring for Your People Like Family.* New York: Penguin Random House, 2015.

Chapter 22

1. "The Birkman Method." Birkman.com. n.d. https://birkman.com/the-birkman-method/.

2. "Reliability and Validity." Birkman.com. n.d. https://birkman.com/the-birkman-method/reliability-and-validity/

Wrap-Up For Principle #3

1. Elliott, Brian. "Rewiring how we work: building a new employee experience for a digital-first world." Slack.com. October 7, 2020. https://slack.com/blog/transformation/remote-employee-experience-index-launch

2. "Leveling the playing field in the hybrid workplace." Future Forum. January, 2022. https://futureforum.com/wp-content/uploads/2022/01/Future-Forum-Pulse-Report-January-2022.pdf

ACKNOWLEDGMENTS

While the cover of this book has a single name on it there are many people over many years that provided the encouragement, experience, knowledge, and impetus to finally make this long-time dream a reality. I will start with the most recent assembly of people and work backwards as that is how my brain works!

First, to my editor Peter Lundell. God is so good that he provided a remarkable man who can do it all when it comes to editing. My first completed manuscript that I sent to him came back with some nice accolades in the beginning but then the gut-punching reality of, "You lost me in the middle part of the book, and you never delivered on your promise!" Ouch did that hurt. But he spoke truth in love, and I went back to work, and the final product is something that I can be very proud of. Thank you, Peter. You are a genius!

To the rest of my book team that consisted of my book coach Cathy Fyock, publishing team of Everett O'Keefe, Chris Simmons, Malia Sexton, Charlie Wormhoudt, and my media/marketing team led by Stephanie Feger and Sandy Wiles from the Empower PR Group, many thanks for the guidance and expertise to help make this a reality. One of my themes is, "the sum of us is greater than any one of us," and that has certainly been true of this endeavor. For those that have written books you know that it takes a tribe, but for those that haven't you have NO idea the amount of effort and heavy lifting that is needed, and all of these folks have made the journey a success.

I would be remiss at this point if I didn't call out my dear friend Nancy Ahlrichs as she is someone who encouraged me to get going and write the book and referred me to her friend and ultimately my book coach Cathy Fyock. Cathy and her team are amazing, and she helped me get to that proverbial "next level" in my writing. It's a reminder that we're all only one person away from meeting the next right person to assist our success!

After I started my first coaching and consulting company in 2009, I never thought that I would go back as a leader for another company that wasn't mine, but God had other ideas and it was His plan that I arrived at IMPACT Group in the summer of 2014 as its president. Thank you, Lauren Herring, for trusting me with your company and our employees, and for letting me drive a vision for our lines of business. Your faith in me was remarkable and what we achieved together will always hold a special place in my heart and mind.

I worked alongside and developed relationships with some of the most incredible people that I've ever worked with while at IMPACT Group. Of course, every executive needs an assistant that makes his or her life easier, and Paige Hite was one of the best. Her bountiful, positive energy and enthusiasm was infectious, and she made coming to the office a joy!

Max Barnett was our CFO while I was at IMPACT Group and he's the best one that I ever worked with. His client focus trumped his need for exactness, and he made doing business with our clients easy and effortless. He always erred on the side of our clients and our people when it came to contracts, pricing, and pay. His support of me and my efforts was exemplary and provided a secure base environment for me to play to win!

Marcie Mueller, our VP Global Leadership Development practice leader, and I were joined at the hip, and I learned so much about instructional design and effective leadership programs that elevated my game to greater heights. She is a consummate professional whose high standards rubbed off on me and we proudly provided some of the most highly effective leadership programs the companies that hired us had ever experienced.

Her sidekick Oneida Werger was a true professional as well and ran our coaching teams around the globe with precision. Those two together are a powerhouse and we couldn't have achieved the success that we had in our leadership division without their incredible dedication!

Dan Coffey ran our outplacement practice while I was there and he's a man of God with high integrity who lifted me up countless times when I needed it. I always knew that Dan had my back and was praying for me. He truly has a servant's heart and the clients that he served always raved about his professionalism and the quality of his effort and work.

And at IMPACT Group I had two of the most incredible sales and client relationship people in Bridget Kadolph and John Gruender. I thanked God for them every day that I was there, and just like Dan and Marcie, they bought into the vision and delivered exceptional results while we worked together. Their support and encouragement were priceless. And then our international representative Tracy Kautzman whose energy and passion for our relocation business and our customers was second to none. Her support greatly enhanced my time there and, of course, I always loved going to Switzerland to work with her. Christina Callahan is their VP of HR and she and I had worked together at TALX Corporation earlier. Christina was a huge supporter of my efforts at IMPACT Group, and it was inspiring to watch her growth and work alongside her twice in my career. Jackie Engel came into IMPACT Group as I was leaving, and she and I also worked at TALX together and we've been long time friends and supporters of each other. She has a unique marketing mind and is a huge asset to IG.

There are many others at IMPACT Group that I admired and worked with such as Kristy Fairbanks, Eric Laegler, Tanya Fite, Ed Marshall, Cathy Williams, Ann Herring, Kim Boyce, Stephanie Eisenstein, and Terry Bellert. I know that I am missing some people at IG that I admire and that were my supporters, but I can't name the entire employee list!

While I've been on my journey as an international leadership consultant and executive coach, I had the benefit of finding friendships and partnerships along the way. One of the first people that provided the encouragement to become a coach is John Arnold. He's one of the best executive coaches on the planet and I'm not sure I would have headed down that path without his encouragement. My certifications in coaching were completed through CoachU and my mentor coach Jille Bartolome, MCC was the best! She guided me through both the ACC and the PCC certification brilliantly.

My first consulting and coaching company found several people joining me in that endeavor. Martin Taylor, who had been a client of mine at TALX while he was with UPS, has become a great friend and he hung his consulting shingle with me from the beginning of that venture. Lisa Dominisse joined as well, and we've continued our friendship and our working relationship in her current CEO role as we both ended up in Indiana after meeting through work in 2005 when she lived in Nebraska. Also, during this timeframe, Carla Street and I partnered on some projects and her genius in brain-based leadership has had a huge influence on my work and thinking, as you will read about in the book.

In 2010 I had the pleasure of joining an international organization, and on a trip to China met Dr. George Kohlrieser. He invited me to attend his High Performance Leadership program at IMD in Lausanne, Switzerland and upon completion then invited me to begin coaching in the program. To say that experience has had a huge influence on me is an understatement. I learned so much about coaching and what it really takes to effect transformation and I will be forever grateful to George for giving me the opportunity to work in that incredible executive development program.

I worked alongside some unbelievably dedicated people at IMD with Cristina Couto being the gem on top of the ring! Her attention to detail and her ability to manage and juggle so many balls for each program is beyond description. My coach when I attended the program, who has become a great friend and supporter, was Joyce Crouch. She is a masterful coach and an even better human being! Her business partner Sharon Busse is also someone I worked with at IMD, and she too has become a great friend. There are so many wonderful coaches and professors that I worked with for the almost ten years that I coached at IMD. One of the best is Jakob van Wielenk who has gone on to establish his own brand and does tremendous work in the area of loss and grief. Susan Goldsworthy and Duncan Coombe were coaching with me in the beginning, and both now have significant leadership roles at IMD. The other coaches I worked with were Andreas Neuman, Jean Pierre Heininger, Nina Merrins, Jaya Machet, Olle Bovin, Josephine Schoolkate, Renee Dineen, Christine Reverchon Masclet, Paul Hunter, Matthew Fairless, Jasmine Chevallez, Aparna Dogra, Marie O'Hara, Paco Soler and Ed Wareing. All of them are extraordinary coaches and even better people!

I'm sure that I've left off a few names in the above list and there are two more that I want to single out from my time working at IMD—Isobel Heaton and Alejandro Altieri. Coaching in the HPL program requires a tremendous amount of focus, organization, and the ability to hold a group of six or seven executives in a small group for six days and evenings to guide them to dig deep and get what they came for from the program. You don't do that the first few times without a lot of support and both Isobel and Alejandro were my secure bases as I learned the ropes and enhanced my coaching knowledge and skills.

The HPL program also provided an opportunity to meet other people that spoke or led sessions. Peter Meyers was teaching the communications module when I first started coaching at IMD and he's a master at his craft. I learned a lot from him and some of his team, like Jeff Raz.

Terry Small was teaching us about the brain when I first started coaching at IMD and he has become a life-long friend and supporter of my efforts. He really knows how to educate and entertain a group of people with the latest on brain-based leadership and information. Jamie Andrew is also someone that I came to know and admire as he came to each session to tell the dramatic story of his mountain tragedy in 1999 when he lost his dear friend, also named Jamie, when a five-day horrific snowstorm came from nowhere to trap them on the mountain. Jamie's daring rescue off the mountain of Le Droit is still considered one of the most dramatic rescues in the history of the Alps. His story of overcoming losing both hands and both legs below the knees and still having a productive life gave everyone a beacon of hope of what is possible no matter what obstacles you faced. I have deep admiration for Jamie.

Then there are the many people that I worked with at TALX Corporation for over 13 years that I'd like to mention. First is Bill Canfield, who was our Chairman and CEO, who you'll have read about in the book, and about the incredible opportunity he provided for me that catapulted me into another stratosphere in the leadership arena. Bill's belief in my abilities will always be appreciated. One of my very best friends came from working there—Doug Kennedy and I were connected in so much of our thinking and how we approached leadership and life. He challenged me at times and vice versa, as, at one point I worked for him and then later he worked for me! He and his family are very dear to me, and his devout Christian faith has always been something that I've admired.

I must also acknowledge Mike Smith, who had a key executive role at TALX. Mike and I met when I had a previous role with another company and when the opportunity appeared to go to work for TALX I reached out to Mike and came away with the belief that if the company was good enough for Mike it was certainly good enough for me! He is a man of deep faith in God and impeccable character and integrity and someone that I admire. I appreciated his support in ever increasing roles that I took on at TALX.

In the early days at TALX there were many people that I worked with and many of them remain friends today. Dave Fowler is someone that I admire as he shifted his roles at TALX many times and helped us continue to elevate and reinvent our services and products. Robert Bell and I worked closely together in different roles and at one point he and I led our Work Number sales team together. There are so many people from that time that I admire. The best HR person I ever worked with was Ellen Stanko. Brian Garcia was our CTO and he and his team did the heavy lifting as we grew our company beyond what many of us could have imagined early on in our endeavors. From that timeframe, here are others that I want to acknowledge: Jackie Engel, Amy McDonough White, Nancy Cragg, Ron Francois, Dara Brenner, Gail Staub, Gary Gremminger, Paul Kooistra, John Williams, Tom Werner, Gene Debons, Kristin Harty, Scott Sherwin, Rob Holloway, Debbie Meyerpeter, Don Kehr, Jim Canfield, Matt

Johnson, Paul Carlson, Tammy Mullin, Mike Andrews, Rosie Biundo, Gary Gremminger, Jeff Knott, Steve Williams, Tom Fischer, Ron Francois, Josh Lang, Mike Dobbins, John Williamson, and Keith Graves. Keith warrants special mention as he became our CFO and did a remarkable job of driving our company toward fiscal responsibility and success!

Janet Ford and I worked together in different roles, and she was always the consummate professional who I could rely on to give me that point/counterpoint opinion of what we were doing or where we were going.

One of her direct reports early in our acquisition binge was Mark Wood and the two of us worked closely together on reinvention after he joined our company when we purchased his. Mark was a huge supporter of my efforts and remains a great friend today. One other key person that came to us through acquisition was Lou Reavis. Lou was the most incredible client services VP that our company had, and her work ethic was second to none. The final person on the team of the regional alignment we had at the time was Steve Schnare. Steve headed up our client services in the Midwest region and was exemplary in how he performed. That team of Robert, Lou, Janet, Steve, and Mark made the work we were doing incredibly inspiring and productive, and I couldn't have had a better team by my side.

When I moved into the role as President of our unemployment cost management division, Ann O'Dell became my administrative assistant. Ann was, and probably still is, the best administrative assistant that any executive could have. Her attention to detail and her willingness to do whatever it took made my life a lot easier. Because of her dedication to do things the right way there were many times that I would have to fuss at her and tell her to go home! I might have saved my breath though as she wouldn't leave until she got what she was working on "just right!"

The team of leaders that I either inherited or appointed at that time became incredibly supportive and productive as we ultimately integrated seven cultures into our one division. Joyce Dear was my VP and there is no way that we could have had the success that we had without her leadership. Joyce was the yin to my yang in that she could manage the details of the business that allowed me to be the vision and inspiration for the division. She supported so many of my ideas and efforts, the most important being the investment in leadership development for all our employees.

The rest of the team was led by some I've already mentioned—Lou Reavis, Steve Schnare, and Mark Wood—but Lynn Marty, Kathy Alu, Mike Mohr, Dan Tienes, and ultimately Robert Lawter rounded out our leadership team. Together we achieved tremendous success and that allowed me to be free to develop into the leader that I had longed to be and believed that I could be. Other people that warrant a mention during this time are Ken Rodini, Cyndy Keaton, Sheila Gramman, Carrie Wingert, Mark Schwendemen, and Sheldon Jackson.

I know that I am leaving off many people on our leadership team during the run of success as President of the unemployment division. There were many regional leaders and team members that helped us achieve the level of success that we had, and I am forever indebted to them for their contributions to the company and their support of my leadership.

Along the journey of life and ultimately the reinvention of who I was as a person, husband, father, and leader, God provided a spiritual mentor at a critical point in my life. Dr. Bill Bennett arrived and shepherded me and my family as we renewed our faith in God and Christ. Dr. Bennett was the most authentic and real spiritual leader I've ever experienced. He's no longer with us, but his impression on me is still with me today. One other person that is still in my life today is Dr. Marcy Hardy. She was our counseling pastor at our church in Marietta and her belief in me and my family is still with us as she has remained a dear friend and advisor.

And I must call out two of my best friends—Dick Stevens and Larry Powell. Dick has been my friend for over 40 years, and we've failed and succeeded together in many ventures. He has stood by me and protected me when I needed it the most. He became great friends with Larry, who I had known since the eighth grade and the three of us formed a new bond that was very special. Unfortunately, Larry received the diagnosis of AML (acute myeloid leukemia) in January, 2020 and he passed away in August of that year. Dick and I went to Charleston many times in 2020 to help his sister Faye take care of him as he tried valiantly to overcome the disease. That was actually a gift that Covid gave me—the ability to not be so busy with work that I was able to spend a significant amount of time with Larry before he passed. We will always remember him when we hear the song "Sweet Home Alabama" or do shots of Fireball!

Finally, a few of my family members that are near and dear to me. My sister Carol bears a special mention as she and I have been close most of our lives and she has been a huge supporter and encourager to me. My uncle Bill Dickey, who is no longer with us, saw something in me early on that inspired me, and his wife, my Aunt Doby, always loved me and supported me as well, even though as teenagers she thought I was a bad influence on her two kids! Speaking of, Fran Griffiths, their daughter, and my most dear cousin, has always been a friend and champion of me and we are kindred spirits in so many ways! In fact, I started writing this book in her home in downtown Charleston in February, 2020. Her brother Ron, of course also my cousin, has been a great friend through the years and we almost always call each other on our birthdays. He and I still think we're 18 years old and act like it when we talk to each other.

And, to my nephews and niece, Ethen, Jordan, and Zach Chaffin, and Brian and Angela Ramsey, thank you for letting me be a friend and mentor to all of you as you've grown and developed through the years. I'm very proud of you and it's been a huge blessing to be alongside you on your journeys.

I know that I have left off people that should be mentioned, but at some point, I must stop naming people or I'm going to write every name of every person with whom I had any kind of relationship with and that would fill another book! If you've read this far, congratulations on helping me acknowledge many people that have influenced, encouraged, and invested in me as a person and a leader. And if you've made it to this point and you believe that you should have been mentioned here, please accept my apologies! Send me an email and let me know that fact and when we do a reprint or revision of the book, I'll see what I can do to mention you next time!

ABOUT THE AUTHOR

Ed Chaffin is the CEO and Founder of The UnCommon Leadership® Institute, LLC. He founded the institute to live out his passion for changing the world one life at a time by helping leaders and their teams be the best version they can be through examining where they've been, where they are, and where they are going! Ed is a seasoned executive, speaker, author, and entrepreneur with years of experience in the HR and talent development arenas.

Ed's rich career history includes being part of the executive team of three companies that he helped build, and his successful corporate career included being President of the largest division of TALX Corporation's (now Equifax Workforce Solutions) unemployment services division serving 9,000 clients and 1,200 employees. He was also President of IMPACT Group, based in St. Louis where through his and his team's leadership they were able to successfully launch a global leadership development division. Ed's experience as an executive led him to a career as an international leadership consultant and executive coach, supporting the development of aspiring leaders and executives.

He has worked with leaders and teams from around the world through his workshops, speeches, and team programs whereby he shares the knowledge and expertise on leadership that has been codified in this book.

Ed has coached more than 300 executives, as well as worked with numerous companies, their leaders, and their teams to bring them into better and stronger alignment and a higher level of performance. He worked for almost ten years as an executive coach at IMD—The International Institute of Management and Development (Lausanne, Switzerland) in their High Performance Leadership (HPL) executive development program. IMD has been ranked the #1 open enrollment university for many consecutive years by the Financial Times. HPL is the #1 program at IMD. He has worked with leaders and teams from over 20 different countries, and companies such as Schindler Elevator, Munich Re, Chegg, Anomali, State Fund, Adveq, Home Depot, and several Silicon Valley start-ups.

He is a Professional Certified Coach (PCC) from the International Coach Federation, an SEIP-certified Coach from The Social and Emotional Intelligence Institute, a Senior Birkman Certified Consultant and holds a certification in Brain Based Leadership. He has affiliations with three major universities where he has taught leadership in master's and MBA programs at Louisiana State University and the University of Missouri, and IMD as previously mentioned.

Ed can be reached at: www.edchaffin.com

www.ingramcontent.com/pod-product-compliance
Lightning Source LLC
Chambersburg PA
CBHW071556210326
41597CB00019B/3277